DECIBEL AMPLIFIED:
BREAKING THE SILENCE OF EXCLUSION

DECIBEL AMPLIFIED: BREAKING THE SILENCE OF EXCLUSION

BY

Dr. U. S. SARANYA

KALPAZ

First Published, 2018

Published by

Kalpaz Publications
C-30, Satyawati Nagar,
Delhi – 110052
Ph.: 011-47034999, 9811692060
www.kalpazpublications.com
E-mail: kalpaz@hotmail.com

Printed at: G. Print Process, Delhi

Cataloging in Publication Data—DK
Courtesy: D.K. Agencies (P) Ltd. <docinfo@dkagencies.com>

Saranya, U. S., author.
Decibel amplified: breaking the silence of exclusion/ by Dr. U.S. Saranya.
pages cm
ISBN 9789386397812 (HB)

1. Indic literature (English)—20th century—History and criticism.
2. Indic literature (English)—21st century—History and criticism.
3. Dalits in literature. I. Title.

LCC PR9489.6.S27 2018 | DDC 820.9954 23

Dedication

This book is dedicated to my Dear parents Mr. G. Sadhasivam and Mrs. S. Umarani the lifeline of my life. I owe my life to them.

Contents

Preface

The Dalit literature as well as its cultural aesthetics is not given legitimate space and not rightly represented in Indian English Literature by the mainstream writers. It is during the postcolonial India especially after 1970s, there are numerous texts and resources available for those who want to pursue their studies on Dalit literature. Dalit literature has got prominent significance in the academic world, as an alternative literature to Indian English Literature. Like the black and natives literatures in America, Canada, New Zealand, Australia and other parts of the world, Dalit literature paved the way for studying the life aspects of the Dalits in India as well as in other countries like Pakisthan, Bangladesh, Srilanka in the South Asia. Irrespective of the exclusion from the mainstream disciplines in Indian universalities during the colonial and the postcolonial periods, the Dalit literature has its own significant existence in enriching and empowering the Dalits across India. It is due to the authentic contribution of the Dalit scholars who are now writing in English as well as translating the Dalit literary texts from regional languages and Hindi into English. The translation of the Dalit texts from regional to global and other national languages paved the way for an authentic critical analysis by the scholars across the world. At this point, the contribution by the conscious non-Dalit academicians and critics who translated and introduced at least some of the themes of the Dalit literature into the academic world will not be ignored.

Now across the country scholars and critics pursue their research on Dalit literature from different perspectives. Presently much research is being done on Dalit literature from the perspectives of comparative literature, translation, gender studies. Dalit literature is also studied in the light of contemporary theories like Postcolonialism, Postmodernism, Marxism, Deconstruction, New-historicism, Psychoanalytical and Feminism. In the backdrop of Ambedkar s concept of *Annihilation of Caste* and Kanshirams concept of *Political Power* for the Dalits, the Dalit literature interfaces other disciplines like philosophy, sociology, culture studies, journalism and mass communication. Studying Dalit literature in the light of fine arts and eco-criticism are some of the remarkable developments of the day.

Dalit Novel is something that deviates from western as well as Indian way of understanding novels. Western novel is in the backdrop of Greek literature similarly Indian novel is in the backdrop of Sanskrit literature. The question is both the Greek influenced Western novel and the Sanskrit oriented Indian novel are of certain exclusions. They exclude the natives and ignore their culture. As a remedy, we see the arrival of native writings like Afro-American, Native Canadian, Aboriginal Australian and Dalit writings in India with similar dialectics in representing their culture in their idiom and now we call them as the native or the fourth world literatures. As a fact, they deal with their folklore, language and present through their novels that the culture of the natives is not subservient to that of the elitists.

The Dalit novel deviates from its Indian English novel because the Indian English novel is highly influenced by the Sanskrit and confines to its conventional norms of representing the country. Instead, the Dalit novel is full of its folklore, consisting of Dalit idiom and glorifying the rich heritage of Dalits and their culture. Another issue that deviates the Dalit novel from that of Indian English novel is that the Dalit novel offers multiple narratives consisting of stories within a story so as the totality of the narration is accepted by the reader. The Dalit novel has no fixed set of rules like that of the Western as well as the Indian English novels. The Dalit novel is simple in structure and setting, common man and women as its protagonists and committed to explore the bare realities of religious rigidity and Caste based limitations that the Dalits experience in their own land for more than four thousand years.

The resonance of the Dalit novel lies in its setting. The characters are common people and not of aristocratic class. They converse about the common issues. Coming to the setting, one can see the characters involve in conversation at cowshed, at church, at Village Panchayat, in the fields or where their fellow Caste people come across each other. The Dalit novel doesnt follow the three unities of time which is a conventional method adopted by the Indian English novel. The Dalit novel presents the events unevenly as per the demand of the situation.

The Dalit novel makes the reader understand that insecure childhood, ever dependence for the assistance of the Government and its welfare policies, Socio-cultural oppression, gender dominance, exploitation in paying the daily wages, sexual harassment at the work places and physical attacks, police cases and political influence are the day to day experiences of the Dalits. The Dalits are left with no option than depending on the Caste Hindus. We can also see the Dalit characters are passive once theymove away from their living areas to that of the Caste Hindus. The experience of alienation and otherness are common issues in the Dalit novel. The Dalit novel succinctly depicts the aspects of the social exclusion and the cultural dominance that the Dalits experience due to the oppressive Hindu social order.

The protagonist of a Dalit novel is an ordinary man or woman of the Dalit community. The protagonist of a Dalit novel should not be a well-educated, rich or employee instead he or she is the one who takes a righteous stand for developing his or her own Caste people. In spite of all odds, the protagonist of the Dalit novel is the one who readily faces the challenges, determines himself or herself to educate and empower his or her people. The protagonist stands as a role model for his Caste. In fact the true protagonist of the Dalit novel is the one who redeems himself or herself to take the lead so as to enlighten the Dalit community by being identified as the one inside the community. At this point I believe the true protagonist of the Dalit novel is the Dalit community itself as the central character merely takes the role of messenger.

Apart from dealing with the above mentioned issues, the Dalit novel also deals with the rich experiences of the Dalits and paved the way for the formation for their collective consciousness rightly identifying themselves to fight against the Caste and Gender hierarchy.

Foreword

Dr. U. S. Saranya's work "Decibel Amplified: Breaking the Silence of Exclusion" is yet another contribution in the ever growing discourse on Dalit Studies. She critically explores the issues of caste inequality, marginalisation, alienation, humiliation and varied Dalit experiences across languages so as to bring out an authentic depiction of Dalit life narratives. Though the Dalit literature has got its momentum and moved beyond its continental limitations, all the other forms of Dalit genre are not scrupulously studied and much contribution is limited to the study of autobiography and poetry. At this point, it is unavoidable issue of present discussion that the significance of studying the Dalit novel similar to that of autobiography and poetry is the need of the day. Dalit novel, similar to the other Dalit genres like personal narratives (autobiography), short stories and poetry, has its own aesthetic values and critical outlook in depicting the Dalits life style. The significance of the Dalit life world is vivid and can be pertinently (re)viewed provided one does an authentic research on Dalit novel. The present proposal is one among such authentic research problems of studying Dalit novel in English translation and its thematic concerns. Dr. U.S. Saranyas work will be considered as an important contribution to the cause of Dalit novel and it would help the researchers and scholars who work on the areas of Caste, Gender and Marginalisation.

Mrs. N.R. Lavanya

Head and Assistant Professor
PG and Research Department of English
Bharathidasan College of Arts and Science
Erode

Acknowledgements

Most importantly, I express my earnest sense of love and gratitude to my dear and loving parents Mr. G. Sadhasivam and Mrs. S Umarani whose vision made me realise the true value of education. I would like to thank them for inculcating and motivating me to have a vision to achieve big and giving me the freedom to learn and grow as an individual. I extend my love and gratitude to my dear aunty Mrs. S Devi Bala who always cares gracefully, loves unconditionally and supports me in every walk of my life and Uncle Mr. K. Shankar Velu. I would like to thank my brother U.S. Prassanna Raj and my dear sister in law Dr. P. Lakshmi for providing necessary feedback and encouraging comments which helped me bring this book out effectively. My heartfelt gratitude to SASTRA University and my sincere thanks to VIT family Dr G Viswanathan, Chancellor VIT University, the Vice Presidents, Assistant Vice President Kadambari S. Viswanathan, Vice Chancellors Dr. Anand Samuel VIT Vellore and Dr. P. Gunasekaran, and Registrars Dr. K. Sathyanarayanan VIT Vellore and Dr. R. Padmanaban VIT Bhopal. My special heartfelt gratitude to the techno crat of VIT Chennai and Bhopal Dr. B. Sathis Kumar for being an true icon and role model for young aspirants.At this juncture, I should sincerely thank the Kalpaz Publishers for their generosity to publish this compilation into a book form. I am deeply indebted to my publishers.

Chapter – I

State wise Critical view of Dalit Literature and its perspectives

Dalits are the people who have been oppressed, culturally subjugated and politically marginalised. Human made the caste system and assigned certain individual to be forced into certain hierarchical status through Hindu religious beliefs. There are four principal caste and the people who fall out of it are called as Dalits. Forming the lower strata of the society they face discrimination in all levels of the society. Right from their rights to education, way of life style, and recruitment in jobs is decided by the upper caste people. Dalits constitutes one third of the population and within the Dalits there are sub-castes as per their works schedule. They do all menial jobs such as leather workers, street sweepers, cobblers, agricultural workers, and manual scavengers. Even after the change of the religion their status in the society never changes. Dalits are found all over the world. The proposition of this paper is to bring out the state wise views of the Dalits from the critics and their way of leading life in this caste, religious and gender dominated environment.

Key words: Dalits, religion, caste, injustice, poverty.

Marati

Eleanor Zelliot traces that the Dalit Sahitya which means the literature of the oppressed in Maharastra is unique "in the quantity of writing, its variety, its aesthetic consideration, its sense of being a movement, its tie to social action, and in the serious attention it receives as a school within the Marathi literary traditions". (1 Mulk Raj Anand & Eleanor Zelliot 1992) Zelliot even states that from Maharashtra the Dalit writing is slowly spreading to other states as Tamil Nadu, Karnataka, Gujarat, Andhra Pradesh and on one day the literature of oppressed will be an all India movement.

Dalit Sahitya started with the movement literature with polemical books, biographies, folk songs, poems, street plays, publishing small booklets about Buddha and Ambedkar. its aim was to distil experience into words, to use language to capture experience and suffering never before recorded. It rarely uses the caste name Mahar, even though most of the poets, novelists and short story writers are former Mahars. It records the history of the movements only when an event such as the burning of the Brahmanical law book, the manusmriti at Mahad in1928 stands as an image for an idea. Arjun Dangle in his article "*Dalit literature: Past Present and Future*" states that the literary movement has today reached various parts of India and the literature is now growing in almost all Indian languages. Yet it is no coincidence that its beginning took place in the Marathi language in Maharashtra. Dr. Ambedkar was from Maharashtra and the Dalit multitudes there supported him fearlessly and loyally. Dr. Ambedkar shaped the tradition of revolutionary thinking almost a generation of Dalits, who can today hold their heads high thanks to him. The literary manifestation of this social awareness is Dalit literature.

Arjun Dangle in his book '*Poisoned Bread'* reveals that Dalit literature came to be used after a stormy discussion organised by the periodical Marathwada in Diwali issue in 1969.... The Dalit literature written by the Dalits and that written by others about the Dalits in Marathi be accepted as a separate entity known as 'Dalit literature' and realizing its cultural importance, the universities and literary organisations should give it a proper place

Meena Kandhaswamy in her article *"A brief history to Dalit literature"* states that Marathi Dalit literature is the forerunner of all modern Dalit literature. It was essentially against exploitation, and made use of writing as a method of propaganda for the movement. It was not immediately recognised by the mainstream which was obsessed with middle class issues.

Punalekar makes an analysis of Dalit writing in Marathi as he writes Dalit literature- short stories, novels, poetry, critical essays, autobiographies, plays, etc. – provides critical insights on the question of Dalit identity. Emerging as a social stream in literary landscape, it tends to cover a wide range of ideas and insights governing the social mindset of Dalits. It also contains a critical evaluation of the prevailing social and cultural practices. He further adds that Dalit writers themselves are either victims of or witness to social inequities and violence. Some have direct or indirect links with social, political and cultural organisations of Dalits A few among them are staunch social activists and often use literature as a vehicle to propagate their view on Dalit identity and prevailing social consciousness. Dalit literature does not constitute a homogenous or unified entity.

Sreekala in her article *"Social consciousness in Dalit writing"* Dalit literature in Maharashtra emerged out of the literary movements which grew out of conversions of Dalits, especially,' Mahars' to Buddhism. Hence this conversion unlike other conversions is remarkable in literature. Marathi Dalit writings of Dalit as well as non-Dalit writers have Buddhist influences in their works. A large number of Dalits who had to undergo opprobrium of public abuse, having to live without self-respect embraced Buddhism which marked a new era in their lives since it gave them new socio-religious and political identity. Though caste consciousness and social differences are subjects of Dalit writings there are other lots many similarities-issues of gender and the question of human dignity. The subjugation of Dalits by the privileged in the name of religion and tradition is delineated in such writings.

Samina Azhar & Vinita Mohindra in their article in muse India titled "*Marathi Dalit literature*" traces about the evolution of Dalit literature in Maharashtra and in general as Dalit literary movement thus has a long history which ideally unfolds the secret struggle against casteist tradition. In modern India, Dalit literature got impetus in Maharastra due to the legacy of Jyotiba Phule (1828-90), Prof. S.M.Mate (1886-1957) and Dr. Ambedkar (1891-1956). With the advent of leaders like Mahatma Phule and Ambedkar in Maharashtra, Who brought forth the issues of Dalits through their work and writings the Dalit movement got a forceful representation. They started a new trend in Dalit writing and inspired many Dalits to come forth with writings in Marathi. Although started in an unorganised way, Dalit literary movement gained pace with the active support of Ambedkar revolutionary ideas which stirred into action all the Dalits of Maharashtra.

Gujarat

Rita Kothari in her introduction in the novel "*The Step Child*" states that since Dalit were the main targets during both the agitations, they felt deeply humiliated and victimized. The educated Dalits felt isolated and alienated. The more articulate among them became more inward looking and their search for self identity led them to deeper explorations of their own collective past. In this intense identity crises, a new Dalit discourse was articulated. It incorporated Dalit history, Dalit Sociology, and above all, Dalit Prose and Dalit Writers."

Joseph Macwan opines that The history of Dalit literature of the last ten years is essentially the history of the expression of the agony experienced by the exploited".

Rita Kothari in the introduction of the translation of the novel "*The Step Child*" Dalit writers mediate with three strands of the Gujarati language representing the three cultures like the literary-classical, the folk-colloquial and the dialectal. As many writers hail from the urban and semi-urban background they are exposed to the native village accent as well as the urban-ghetos. Early poets like Nirav Patel and Dalpat Chauhan weaved the literary and folk elements together, Pravin Gadhvi fused the classical language and the civilisation metaphors, Sahil Parmar spoke the idiom of the urban-ghettos. The arrival of the short stories and novels the writers like Joseph Macwan, Dalpat Chauhan and Mohan Parmar put forth the rural culture through the local dialects. Such expressions lead to the authenticity of the work and "it enriched the Gujarati language by re-establishing the folk against the classical idiom, the 'Parkrit' against the 'Sanskrit'".

Like all Dalit literatures, Gujarati Dalit literature is about assertion of human rights, self-pride, revolt against social injustice, chronicles of personal and collective suffering, and hopes and aspirations for a new society devoid of discrimination. It definitely is a weapon for the struggle; it addresses primarily dalits but the other readers are also considered. As Neerav Patel puts, "I wish you to be not only my reader but also an empathizer, then and only then perhaps my pain would end."

Rameshchandra Parmar, President of Gujarat Dalit Panther and editor of *Panther* and *Akrosh* magazine defines Dalit literature as "that which provides a platform for the formation of casteless and classless society is Dalit literature. It is also necessary that it should also give expression to the exploitation and injustice of the world" (Neerav Patel)

Valjibhai Patel, editor of *Dalit Mitra* magazine and director- activist of council for social justice has the broadest definition: that which portrays reality of human life and its sufferings is Dalit literature.

Praveen Gadhvi another major Dalit poet defines that: "That which artistically expressed the joys and emotions and rights and dignity of the Dalits is Dalit literature"

Bhi Na Vankar defines the idea of Dalit literature as: that which expresses Dalit sensibility and Dalit consciousness is Dalit literature.

Raju Solanki, a young Dalit poet with left-leaning ideology says: that which expresses Dalit sentiments, Dalit consciousness, Dalit sensitivity and has in its centre the Dalit but that which also encompasses the poor and depressed classes of the world is Dalit literature.

Indukumar Jani, editor of Naya Marg, the progressive magazine that has played bigger role in publishing Gujarati Dalit literature has this to offer as definition of Dalit literature: That which express anguish against the present social system, that which aims for change in the unjust social system that which aims for change in the unjust social system, that which protest against the slavish traditions, that which voices the suffering of the depressed classes is Dalit literature.

Chandu Maherriya, editor of *Dalit Adhikar* and activist-journalist says: Dalit does not merely mean scheduled castes. But Dlait is an effort that believes in the equality of all human beings, treats everybody at par, that struggles against inequality. That what is written for human dignity, human rights, and human identity is Dalit literature.

Senior Dalit poet, Dalpat Chauhan vices his opinion as thus: that which expresses sufferings of Dalits, that which guides their aspirations, and that which has negation of god, revolt, unity and equality of man, new awareness is Dalit literature.

Harish Manglam, a poet, novelist and editor, says in an interview published in 'Eklavya with Thumb', another anthology of Gujarati Dalit poetry translations says that literature written about Dalits is Dalit literature but only literature written by writers that come from Dlait communities has the authority of experience and the ring of truth.

Deepak Mehta in the preface to yet another Gujarat Dalit poetry anthology 'Visfot' writes: we should not interpret Dalit literature as the one that is written about Dalits or written by the Dalits. Dalit literature doesn't belong to any particular caste/varna or class. It is the literature that joins the oppressed and exploited of the world, whenever they are, emotionally and rationally.

Neerav Patel states about the emergence of Dalit literature in the blog Gujarat Dalit Sathiya as Dalit literature has reasons to take birth like the incarnation of that Hindu God who announced yada yada hi... To kill the darkness caused by the oppressors of mankind and restore dignity and equality and liberty and fraternity for all human beings that inhabit the earth. One must know how dark is that darkness, that darkness that turns man into slave, man into beast.

Like other Dalit writings, Gujarati Dalit literature is also the product of a revolt against the age-old exploitation and torture of the Gujarati upper castes. Literally, it is a revolt against decadent Modernism in Gujarati Literature. Like other parts in India, Gujarati Dalit literature was also determined and guided by the Dalit Movements in Gujarat. The movement provided a platform for Dalit writers whose creativity received no attention from a parochial literary establishment.

Gujarati Dalit literature in its first phase became synonymous with Dalit poetry as it were and the themes that inspired Dalit poets to wield their pens were revolt, protest, revenge, resentment and disgust against upper caste oppression and exploitation, unjust and enslaving social customs and traditions, most importantly the appropriation of these by the upper castes.

As Joseph Macwan writes in the preface of Asmita' (identity) that the history of Dalit literature of the last ten years is essentially the history of the expression of the agony experienced by the exploited

As K. M. Sherrif observes that the Dalit writing has been described as one of the manifestations of Postmodernism in Indian literatures. However, the acquisition of postmodernist idiom, modes and attitudes has not been uniform in Gujarati Dalit literature. (98-Shodganga)

Dalit literature in Gujarati literary scene entered with a specific purpose. In neighboring Maharashtra, it was an old entrant. Marathi Dalit ideology was framed out of life sketches of Dr. Babasaheb Ambedkar and Jyotiba Phule. But Gujarati Dalit literature never had a privilege to have such powerful leaders. On the other hand even Gandhian ideology also could not influence Gujarati Dalit literature.

The term Dalit Literature has literary, cultural, religious, social, political, historical and economic implications. Like other marginalised literature, especially Black literature and women's writings, Gujarati Dalit literature started off as protest'literature and has been looked upon as oppositional' literature.

K. M. Sherrif states that in Gujarati Dalit writing, for instance, there is the invocation of a subaltern mythology as a foil to Classical Hindu mythology which has served as the bulwark of caste-hegemony for centuries, effectively disfiguring, assimilating or marginalizing sub-cultures outside the pale of the 'mainstream'. There is also a quest for a 'golden age' when 'all men lived as equals' and Dalit ideology and culture were the mainstream. This tendency is less visible in Tamil or Malayalam Dalit writing.

Tamil

Meena Kandhaswamy in her article "*Brief Introduction to Dalit literature*" states that like all other Dalit literature,

Tamil Dalit literature too has an excess of autobiographies. Critics condemn these literatures of lament, but they too have a central place within the creative core. Tamil Dalit literature is characterised by the call for self-identity and assertion. It tramples all conventions with its intensely personal expression; is concerned with the life of the subaltern, and deals out a stark brutality. This literature should be viewed not as a literature of vengeance or a literature of hatred, but a literature of freedom and greatness.

Dalit literature in Tamil voices concern over friction among the various Dalit communities. It points out the Intra-Dalit strife strengthens the hands of the upper caste, landed class and vote garnering politicians... Dalit literature nevertheless, underscores the need to bury differences among the Dalit groups and offer an organised, united resistance to social, political oppression of their community. Dalit writers in Tamil have made effective interventions in formulating in innovative, radical experimentation in linguistic and aesthetic paradigms and have offered challenge to critics who are dismissive of Dalit writing on grounds of traditional aesthetic norms. Dalit writers experiment in terms of genres and expand the limits of literary language to include spoken, conversational, earthy vocabulary of the marginalised. Their use of folklore, legend, myths, swearwords render their narrative closer to everyday life. Dalit writings argue that their work require/merit an alternative aesthetic paradigm that is aware of Dalit lifestyle and experiential realities. The violence that pervades Dalit lives invades their literary expression and they trounce hegemonic, traditional, mainstream literary/aesthetic parameters and surge ahead to formulate a fresh, alternative, innovative, radical literary idiom. Such an exercise leaves its impact on generic as well as linguistic norms.

In 1995 in Tamil *India Today* brought out a special annual issue on Tamil Dalit writing that included Raj Gauthaman's critical essay, stories by Sivakami,

Idayaventhan, Bama, Ravikumar, Cho.Dharmam and Imayam and poetry by K.A.Gunasekaran and Pratibha Jeyachandran. This moment can be *described* as the birth of Dalit writing in Tamil Nadu".

The emergence of the Dalit literature started in Maharashtra and spread like a forest fire to different states like Karnataka, Gujarat, Andhra Pradesh, Punjab, Kerala and Tamil Nadu. Many works were translated and it gained a momentum and various people read the writings which were translated by the non-Dalits. The 'Translation Revolution' which was started in the 1990's introduced the Tamil Dalit Writing in English and it is the first book to focus exclusively on Tamil Dalit writing so far even in its native spheres. Dalit literature traces its origin from the Ancient Buddhist or the medieval anti-caste movement, even before the birth of the word 'Dalit' the literature about the untouchables existed to fight against the discrimination.

Tamil Dalit Literature identifying itself as the literature of protest it found its impact on form and content which frequently influenced the language and styles of the writers. The writers challenged the stereotyped and not only wept, accused, and abused but also laughed, loved and celebrated. The Tamil Dalit writing has produced autobiographies, novels, poems, short stories and got a separate sphere to express the pain and suffering in different forms. It focuses on the enriched content, creative writing with different style and approach.

Karantaka

B.M Puttaiah writes about Dalit literature as it is the literature that captures the desire, dreams, belief, agony, suffering, violence, humiliation, impatience, dissatisfaction, rage and resistance of Dalits. After the Boosa agitation the Dalit created their own space for writings and they did not depend on the conventional Brahmin writers. It not only created Dalit intellectuals but it also brought them together and it inspired the coming generation of writers to.

Malagatti says about the Kannada agitation of the people to get their won space in writing and other walk of life as "it appears that there is no Dalit movement, but it is there, like a river flowing in different directions."

Paramjit S.Judge in his article "*Punjab Dalit literature: Existence, Identity and Beyond*" states about the words of Nagaraj as he identifies two major features of Dalit literature in Karnataka Firstly, it explores the world of the untouchable and other humiliated castes, although the word 'Dalit' means the oppressed in general. Secondly, it is written by members of the class which makes for a crucial difference. Not that such experience was not available earlier in our literature. It was there, but seen outside.... Dalit literature is the product of the new generation who are brilliant and their rejection of the Hindu society is total".

Telugu

Thummapudi Bharati states in his writing for the cause of the emergence of the Dalit literature is "There is a long past in the creation of Dalit consciousness in Telugu Literature. Perhaps the exploitation of life, reaction, pleading, protest, reform, progress and revolution are the causes in the creation of Telugu Dalit literature".

Katti Padma Rao points out the historical foundation of the Telugu Dalit literature as "The hold of caste remained intact; dalit localities became killing fields, habitations of landless poor Dalits were attacked, burnt and looted every day, in a routine manner. But the heroic Dalits rebelled. Dalit literature was born out of this oppression, this caste violence".

Katti Padma Rao says that "it [karamchedu incident] developed several original forms of agitation; it produced some leaders and many activists [writers and singers]. In fact, there is a sense in which the Karamchedu struggle is the foundation for all the recent changes in the attitude and stance of Dalits. Karamchedu massacre is the bench mark in Telugu Dalit literature.

K. Satya Narayan in his article "Category of Class, Caste and Telugu Literature" states that the liberal and traditional Telugu critics advanced an argument that modern Telugu literature is a domain of universal values, whereas Dalit literature is casteist in character and is associated with narrow political goals. R.S. Sudarshanam, the winner of the Sahitya Akademi Award and a reputable literary critic, contends that 'Dalit literature' assumes the character of a political catchphrase and that it is instrumentalised in an attempt to bring caste politics into the literary domain.

Dalit literature has fresh expressive comprehension and distinct intellectual vigour. Its distinctness "lies in its authentic unity of language and content. In it the disillusionment and disgust of young Dalits, often accompanied by a desire for revenge, come alive. it revives the memory of the pain and suffering of the past generations." Further, "it confronts centuries of hypocrisy, deceit and violence sustained in the name of tradition"

Mainstream Telugu literature witnessed another literary trend during the forties called Ahyudaya Sahitvam or progressive literature, in protect against the prevalent romanticism, idealism and traditional individualism. The writings of this school also reflected on the global problems of the economic depression of the thirties and the fascist aggression in Europe. They idealised communism and propagated the communist utopia of world revolution.

Punjab

Paramjit S.Judge in his article "*Punjab Dalit literature: Existence, Identity and Beyond*" states that there are certain unique dimensions of the Punjabi Dalit literature. It should be noted that the emergence of the Dalit literature in Punjabi was not a logical culmination of a collective movement for equality. Sikhism and Marxism played very important role in determining the course of the literary writings in the twentieth century Punjab. He further adds that Dalit literature in Punjab is well established despite its very short history. There is a powerful emergence of the new generation of Punjabi Dlait writers who are not stifled by the overwhelming oppressive structure of the caste society. They are educated and less dependent upon the upper castes. They are engaged in Dalit organisation and movements. They are coming out with a new language providing fresh perspective to the Punjabi literature. The most important aspect in that in a short period of time the diversity in perspective within this type literature has become visible. Thus Dalit literature in Punjabi is going to become more important type of literature in future. He further states that Punjabi Dalit literature should be understood as a part of the Dalit assertion and effervescence in the postcolonial India.

Hindi

Om Prakash Valmiki in his own book in "Hindi on Dalit Aesthetics" states that Dalit literary movement is not just a literary movement. It is also a cultural and social movement. Dalit society has been imprisoned for a thousand years in the dark mist of ignorance, deprived of knowledge. Dalit literature is the portrayal of the wishes and aspirations of these oppressed and tormented Dalits.

According to Valmiki Dalit literature is the literature of masses. It is a literature of action, based on human values, which wages a struggle born out of anger and rebellion against feudalistic mindsets.

R. Sasidharan in his article *"Key-Text in Hindi Dalit literature: A thumbnail Analytical Sketch"* writes that Hindi Dalit author, Omprakash Valmiki, "Dalit consciousness lies not in providing descriptions of the dejections, pains, exploitations and depressions of Dalit people, nor is it a tearful lamentation of the hardships of the Dalits without the intensity of life experience.

Jaiprakash Kardam, another Hindi author, has stated, "Many authors like Premchand, Nirala and Amruthlal Nagur have written a lot about the Dalits. They can't be rejected. However, their writings were 'about Dalit lives'; but they were not written with a Dalit consciousness"3 . There is a great difference between 'literature about Dalit lives' and 'literature of Dalit consciousnesses. In literature about Dalit lives, there is a back-breaking burden of the acceptance of fate and tradition. For Dalits, these traditions were just depressing; they were not something to be cherished. In mainstream Hindi literature, Dalits are not depicted better than beggars.

Malayalam

Dalits presence in Malayalam literature becomes meaningful only when it opens up new vistas of aesthetics.... Dalit is only a common term for designating the untouchables. But the word has a history that they refuse to acknowledge. It became part of the socio-political discourse of the turbulent 1960's, as an epitome of India's dreams of liberation. It carries the weight not only of strife but also of centuries long-philosophical enquiry.

References

Azhagarasan and Ravikumar (2012).The Oxford India Anthology of Tamil Dalit Writing. Oxford University Press, New Delhi, pp. 1-298.

Basu Tapan (2002). Translating Caste. Delhi University, New Delhi, pp. 10-43.

Bharathi Thummapudi (2008). A History of Telugu Dalit Literature. Kalpaz Publication, New Delhi, pp. 13 -237.

Bhosale, B.V. (2014). Sociology of Dalit literature, ABD Publishers, New Delhi, pp. 1- 94.

Dangle Arjun (1994). Poisoned Bread: Translations from Modern Marathi Dalit Literature. Orient Black Swan, Mumbai, pp. 1-325.

Dasan M., V. Pratibha, Pradeepan and Chandrika (2011).The Oxford Anthology of Malayalam Dalit Writing. Oxford University Press, New Delhi, pp. 5-290.

Kumar Raj (2010). Dalit Personal Narratives: Reading Caste, Nation andIdentity. Orient Blackswan, New Delhi, pp.1-55.

Limbale Sharankumar (2004). Towards the Aesthetics of Dalit Literature: History, Controversies and Considerations. Orient Black Swan, Hyderabad, pp. 1-40.

Michel, S.M. (2007). Dalits in Modern India Vision and Values.Sage publications, New Delhi, pp. 1-360.

Mohanty Manoranjan (2004). Class, Caste and Gender. Sage Publication, New Delhi, pp. 1-154.

Nagaraj, D.R. (2010). The Flamming Feet and other essays: The Dalit Movement in India. Permanent Black, New Delhi, pp. 6-47.

Nimbalkar Waman (2006). Dalit literature: Nature and Role. Prabodhan Prakashan, Nagpur, pp. 1-53.

Satyanarayana and Susie Tharu (2011). No Alphabet Insight: New Dalit writing from South India. Penguin, New Delhi, pp. 1-81.

Satyanarayana and Susie Tharu (2013). Steel Nibs are Sprouting: New Dalit writing from South India. Harper & Collins, Uttar Pradesh, pp. 1-45.

Chapter - II

Origin of Novels in English and Evolution of Dalit Novels:
A Critical Study

Literature as a form emerged in English during the Elizabethan rule. From there on it spread to different countries and people started to have their own literature as a mode of expressing their socio-cultural aspects. The proposition of the paper is to trace the beginning of the Novel form in England and then how it set roots in Indian English literature as a genre and finally to Dalit literature in expressing the authentic and realistic mode of expression of their way of life.

Keywords: Novel, English, origin, evolution, self-expression

The modern English literature began in 16th century during the reign of Queen Elizabeth.The restoration of the king Charles II to the throne in 1660 ushered to a new age known as the age of reason. This restoration period and the 18th century with the writers like Dryden, Pope, Johnson and Goldsmith are marked the way of Augustus age in the literature. This period revives the classical and the neoclassical literature. It was in this period that the birth of English novel took place. Samuel Richardson was the first to introduce this form with his first novel *Pamela.* Next to him came Henry Fielding with his great novel *Tom Jones* then many novelists like Tobias Smollet with his work *Humphery Clinker* and Laurence stern author of *Tristram Shandy* became famous for their works in novel form. Daniel Defoe is often given the credits for the discovery of the modern novel.

Victorian Age is marked with the rapid and radical changes in the Scientific and industrial world though the novel as a form emerged in the Augustus age but it gained its momentum in the Victorian period with eminent and noteworthy novelist. Females started writing in this age and Victorian age is considered to be mainly the age of Novel. It became an increasingly popular literary form. Novel as a form moved from a mere story-telling to subtle craft by choosing the realistic individual problem and representing it through novels. In the modern age James Joyce is considered to be the pioneer in the field of novel.

Terry Eagleton in her book "The English Novel an Introduction" states that a novel is a piece of prose fiction of a reasonable length...The truth is that the novel is a genre which resists exact definition...The point about the novel, however, is not just that it eludes definitions, but that it actively undermines them. It is less a genre than an anti-genre. It cannibalizes other literary modes and mixes the bits and pieces promiscuously together...You can find poetry and dramatic dialogue in the novel, along with epic, pastoral, satire, history, elegy, tragedy and any number of other literary modes. Virginia Woolf described it as 'this most pliable of all forms'. It is the queen of literary genres in a rather less elevated sense of the word than one might hear around Buckingham Palace. The novel is an anarchic genre, since its rule is not to have rules. An anarchist is not just someone who breaks rules, but someone who breaks rules as a rule, and this is what the novel does too. Myths are cyclical and repetitive, while the novel appears excitingly unpredictable. In fact, the novel has a finite repertoire of forms and motifs. But it is an extraordinarily capacious one even so.

Mikhail Bakhtin, the novel tends to emerge and disappear again, like a river threading its way through a limestone landscape. Bakhtin is surely right to see the novel as emerging from the stream of culture dripping with the shards and fragments of other forms. It is parasitic on the scraps and leavings of 'higher' cultural life-forms; and this means that it has only a negative identity. In its mixing of languages and forms of life, it is a model of modern society, not simply a reflection on it.

Hegel saw the novel as the epic of a prosaic modern world. It has all the range and populousness of the epic, without, for the most part, its supernatural dimension. The novel resembles the classical epic in its consuming interest in narrative, dramatic action and the material world. It differs from it, however, in being a discourse of the present rather than of the past.

As the word 'novel' would suggest. But it also means that the novel's authority is ungrounded in anything outside itself, which is what renders it precarious. In this sense, the novel is a sign of the modern human subject. It, too, is 'original', in the sense that modern men and women are supposed to be the authors of their own existence. Who you are is no longer determined by kinship, tradition or social status; instead, it is something you determine for yourself. Modern subjects, like the heroes of modern novels, make themselves up as they go along. They are self-grounding and self-determining, and in this lies the meaning of their freedom. It is, however, a fragile, negative kind of freedom, which lacks any warranty beyond itself. There is nothing in the actual world to back it up.

For many eighteenth-century commentators, the answer to the question 'What is a novel?' would be: 'A trashy piece of fiction fit only for servants and females'. On this definition, Jackie Collins writes novels but William Golding does not. For these early observers, the novel was less like the The

Times than the News of the World. It was also like a newspaper because it was a commodity you usually bought and read only once, as opposed to the more traditional practice of possessing a small clutch of edifying works which you perused over and over again.

Novel the older kinds of narratives—sometimes called romances—looked at life through distorting lenses and portrayed idealised, implausible characters, the novel, we are told, turned its attention to the ordinary lives of real people in the real world. In this article the four factors about the novel are discussed they are First, narratives are about human beings, the ideals and norms that guide their lives, the passions that drive them, and the action they take. Second, novels portray individuals in different ways, as strong souls, sensitive hearts, or enigmatic psyches. Third, while literary and, more generally, artistic genres are linked to the social and intellectual life of their time, they also enjoy a qualified autonomy. Fourth, although individual decisions play an important role in the evolution of literature, the history of the novel does not consist in great writers relentlessly pushing the genre forward.

Meriam Webster's Dictionary gives definition of the novel as an invented prose narrative that is usually long and complex and deals especially with human experience through a usually connected sequence of events

Oxford Dictionary's definition of the novel is A fictitious prose narrative of book length, typically representing character and action with some degree of realism.

Timothy Spurgin in his book "The English novel" describes novel as "A great novel often seems to describe an entire society, creating a vivid image of the relationships among whole classes of people. It's no wonder that novels are frequently described as the forerunners of modern ethnographies and social histories.... novels are free to probe the inner recesses of both mind and heart. By the end of a novel, we may have developed a deep sympathy and, perhaps, some kind of identification with the characters. In addition to examining human communities, then, the novel explores the nature of consciousness itself. (1-Timouthy-2006)

Fiction, being the most powerful form of literary expression today, has acquired a prestigious position in Indian English literature. It is generally agreed that the novel is the most suitable literary form for the exploration of experiences and ideas in the context of our time, and Indian English fiction occupies its proper place in the field of literature. Prof. M. K. Naik remarks:

> ...one of the most notable gifts of English education
> to India is prose fiction for though India was
> probably a fountain head of story-telling, the novel
> as we know today was an importation from the West

The Indian English fiction is divided into three phases they are the beginning Phase 1930, the period between 1930 and 1980 and the final phase after 1980. The novel form has its origin from the west and in India the country was known for its epics and tales. The Indian English novel narrates the greatness of Indian civilisation and about the past history of the country. The first proper Indian English novel originated in the year 1864 *Rajmohan's Wife* by Bankimchandra Chatterjee. Rabindranth Tagore contributed many of his works to the Indian English literature some of his works are in English already and his immoral literary piece of work is *Gitanjali.* Political themes, religious and historical themes were dealt in the novels. The second period in the Indian English fiction from 1930-1980 is called the second coming of the novels until then more significant writers did not contribute much to the novels. Many national leaders became the icon of representing India like Gandhi, Nehru and Patel. The English critic William Walsh coined the term the Big Threes for the three eminent writers like Mulk Raj Anand, Raja Ram Mohan Roy and R.K.Narayanan. There are many other writers to but these three laid a foundation to the Indian English fiction. The writers of this age depicted the social reality of the society, identity crises, east west domination, and cultural identity into their novels. More of Indianness is embedded into the novel as a form of genre states T.D. Brunton. Modern fiction started to evolve and Spenser remarks that it's the Indianness that prevented the growth of the novel before the arrival of the British in India. After the independence the novelist started to adopt a different form of narration like the stream of consciousness, imagery,new forms of expression, idioms, phrases, and symbols evolved into the novels. After 1980 is considered to be a renaissance period where in the perspective of the postcolonial ideology came into the stream and the realistic portrayal of the nation was seen in the novels. The striking thing about the English fiction after the 1980's is that the playful usage of language they started using local idiom to represent the reality in the country but before that the novelists were so meticulous in writing and they wrote for the English readers.

Pre-Independence Novelist in India

Bijay Kumar Das in his article "Remembering the founding fathers of Indian English Fiction" states that historically Indian English fiction owes its origin to Bankim Chandra Chatterjee's Rajmohan's Wife (1864), its foundation was laid by Mulk Raj Anand when he published his Untouchable in 1935. R.K.Narayan and Raja Rao joined him in giving, as it were, 'a local habitation and a name' to Indian English fiction in nineteen thirties. Anand's Untouchable and Coolie, Narayan's Swami and Friends and The Bachelor of Arts, Raja Rao's Kanthapura mark the beginning of Indian English fiction. And these three novelists continued to write till the end of the twentieth century.

William Walsh says that 'If Anand is the novelist as reformer, Raja Rao is the novelist as metaphysical poet,

Narayan is simply the novelist as novelist' Bijay in his article further traces the importance of the three eminent writers of the Indian English Fiction as Walsh calls R.K.Narayan, 'the novelist as moral analyst. C.D.Narasimhaiah says, "Where distinctions are made they fall into neat categories of Anand the Marxist, progressive or committed writer; Narayan the comic genius or writer pure and simple; and Raja Rao the religious or philosophical novelist (148). These three novelists have broken new grounds in Indian English fiction in terms of making innovations in themes and techniques. They have re-created their characters in their own situations-social, as well as psychological. If Anand is known for humanism, Narayan is known for social and psychological realism and Rao for metaphysical ideas.

Bijay states that Anand was always giving importance to creative literature, highlighting indigenous culture and social art form. He was a rebel in young age and social realism is the main concern in his novels. Anand's important novels include Untouchable (1935), Coolie (1936), Two Leaves and a Bud (1937), The Village (1939), Across the Blackwaters (1941), The Big Heart (1945), Seven Summers (1951), The Private Life of an Indian Prince (1953), Gauri (1960), Morning Face (1968), Confessions of a Lover (1976), The Bubble (1984), Little Plays of Mahatma Gandhi (1991) and Nine Moods of Bharata: Novel of a Pilgrimage (1998).

R.K.Narayanan published his first novel Swami and Friends in the year 1935 and he created a imaginative and fictional place called Malgudi, he is traditional in his representation of the characters in his novel. His novels speaks about the Hindu culture and deep rooted tradition and his notable works are The Bachelor of Arts (1937), The English Teacher (1945), Mr Sampath (1949), The Financial Expert (1952), Waiting for Mahatma (1955), The Guide (1958), The Man Eater of Malgudi (1962), The Vender of Sweets (1967), The Painter of Signs (1977), The Tiger of Malgudi

(1983), Talkative Man (1983), The World of Nagaraj (1990) and Grandmother's Tale (1992).

Raja Rao is the youngest among the trios and he is known for his metaphysic Indian tradition. His important works are Kanthapura (1938), The Serpent and the Rope (1962), Cat and Shakespeare (1965) and The Chessmaster and His Moves (1988). Bijay further states that Anand, Narayan and Rao have many things in common. All 'the Big Three' as William Walsh called them, were influenced by Gandhi and tried to make a myth around Gandhi in their novels. All these three lived abroad, and were exposed to western life and culture. Unlike diasporic writers they never thought of 'imaginary homeland' - they were firmly rooted in India. All of them won Sahitya Akademi Award for their novels - R.K. Narayan for The Guide in 1960, Raja Rao for The Serpent and the Rope in 1963 and Mulk Raj Anand for Morning Face in 1971. (14-Bijay 2009) He further adds that if we compare Anand, Narayan, and Raja Rao with the novelists of nineteen eighties and nineties says, Vikram Seth, Vikram Chandra, Sashi Tharoor, Arundhati Roy, Kiran Nagarkar, Upamanyu Chatterje, and Amitav Ghosh, we find that the great trios have nothing to fear. If these new novelists have made innovations in terms of themes and techniques, the great trios have done that in their own way. (14- Bijay 2009)

The other novel which belong to this period is C.S.Rau's The Confession of the Rogue Patriot 1923, J.Chinnadurai's Sugirtha 1929, Ram Narain's The Tigress of the Harem 1930, H.Kaveribai's Meenakshi's Memoris- A Novel of Christian life in south India 1937, V.V.Chintamani's Vedantham or the clash of the Tradtions 1938, Shankar Ram's The love of Dust 1938, G.F.Karaka's Just Flesh 1941, There lay the city 1942, and we never die 1944, C.N.Zutshi's Motherland 1944, Purushottamadas Tricumdas's living Mask 1947 and N.S. Phadke's Leaves in the August Wind and The Whirlwind.

After Independence

After the advent of the trios like Mulk Raj Anand, R.K. Narayanan and Raja Rao it was the writers like Salman Rushdie who won the booker prize for his novel Mid Night Children. Nayanthra Segal was the first female writer to get wide acclamation she received Sahitya Academy award for her novel Rich like US. Anitha Desai, Kiran Desai, Ruskin Bond, Vikram Seth, Amitiv Gosh, Aravind Adiga, V.S.Naipaul and Arunthathi Rai were notable novel writers in India. Girish Karnad and Mahesh Dattani was great dramatist of India. Poetry excelled with the writings of Rabindranath Tagore and he won the Nobel Prize for his work Gitanjai and other poets were Sarojini Naidu, Toru Dutt and Madhusudhan Dutt. Fiction arrived last in the Indian literary scene.

Post-Independence the Indian novels gained its momentum with the writers like Babahani Battachariyar, Manohar Malgonkar, Kushwanth Singh, Arun Joshi, Chaman Nahal and well known women novelist like Ruth Pawar, Kamala Markandaya, Nayanthra Segal, Jhabvala and Anitha Desai.

The Indian novel in English has come a long way from the triumvirate of the 1930's. The language which was once treated as foreigner, or the language of the elite class, is viewed differently. As the number of the readers has increased so as the quality of writing also improved. The writers are now no longer active users of English but they have English as their first language. They express themselves with native proficiency they are the writers who think and write in one language, which is English. They have travelled in every continent and they have something substantial to tell their readers. Indian English fiction is now the part of world literature. It has struggled endured in the difference of west and now finally emerged as a clear winner among the recent fiction writers.

Now the modern young fiction writers are ruling the Indian English fictions with their best selling and notable works. Writers like Chetan Baghat with his works like One Night at the Call Center, Five point someone, 2 States, Three Mistakes of my Life, Revolution 2020 and Half Girlfriend. Amish (Tripathi) Shiva Triology, Ravinder Singh with his works like I too had a Love story, can love happen twice were the best sellers and youngsters got the habit of reading novels with the writers eminent way of portraying the reality of the young generation in their respective novels.

The Indian English Novels has gone through a lot of transformation from its initial days to its present times and has attained its whole new intensity in terms of concept marketing, presentation, business and impact on Indian Culture.

Dalit Literature in India

Dalit as a word was used in India only after independence by which the Dalits gained inspiration from the pioneers like Jothirao Phule, Bhuddha and Ambedkar. Hinduism as a relion divided man from man and it did not unite them into humanity. The Dalit writers and the writings are real, authentic and lively these are the hall marks of the Dalit literature. The stories of the Dalits are untold and unheard history and to make the unknown know to the world is the emergence of Dalit literature. R. Ramanathan in his article "Studying Dalit literature in Indian writing in English "states that in subaltern studies, oppressed and oppressor. The oppressed want to relieve themselves from the tyrannical clutches of the oppressor, against which the oppressed protest to establish themselves. So, the literature of the subaltern group is usually portrayed as protest literature, in which the oppressed try to release themselves from the clutches of the oppressor.

FEATURES OF DALIT NOVEL

Dalit literature itself is the literature of protest and it gives voice to the voiceless. The originality of the Dalit novel lies in its setting. The characters are common people and not of aristocratic class and they converse about the common issues not about Nation and its Politics. Coming to the setting, one can see the characters involve in conversation at cowshed, at church, at Village Panchayat, in the fields or where their fellow Caste people come across each other. The Dalit novel doesn't follow the three unities of time which is a conventional method applied to study the Indian English novel. The Dalit novel presents the events unevenly and as per the demand of the situation. We find the repetition of the incidents in the Dalit novel.

The Dalit novel makes the reader understand that insecure childhood, ever dependence for the assistance of the Government, Socio-cultural oppression, gender dominance, exploitation in paying the daily wages, sexual harassment at the work places and physical attacks, police cases and political influence are the day to day experiences of the Dalits. We can also see the Dalit characters are passive once they move away from their living areas to that of the Caste Hindus. The experience of alienation and otherness are commonly found incidents in the Dalit novel. The Dalit novel succinctly depicts the aspects of the Social exclusion and the cultural dominance that the Dalit experience due to the oppressive Hindu social order.

Apart from dealing with the above mentioned issues, the Dalit novel is of rich experiences of the Dalits and paved the way for the formation for their collective consciousness rightly identifying themselves to fight against the Caste and Gender hierarchy.

Reference

https://analepsis.files.wordpress.com/2011/08/loganencyclopedianovel.pdf

http://www.english.ufl.edu/mrg/readings/the%20novel.pdf

http://repository.usu.ac.id/bitstream/123456789/27135/4/Chapter%20II.pdf

http://www.creative-writing-now.com/types-of-novels.html

https://www.britannica.com/art/novel/Types-of-novel

http://revisionworld.com/a2-level-level-revision/english/prose/types-novel

http://examples.yourdictionary.com/examples-of-novels.html

http://revisionworld.com/a2-level-level-revision/english/prose/types-novelhttps://www.britannica.com/art/novel#toc50973

http://examples.yourdictionary.com/examples-of-novels.html

http://www.mediatheque-rueilmalmaison.fr/IMG/pdf/engindia.pdf

Chapter - III

"Writing the Rape: A Critical Study of Rape Narratives through Feminist and Dalit Lens"

The historians and the nationalists in India are of the view that women are under ever pressure and subjected to experience the domestic violence. They also claim that India is predominantly a male dominated country and claim that the Indian women are in need of the liberty and freedom and equal opportunities. Dalit women and other women are always being humiliated in body and mind through sexual harassment, domestic violence and rape. For all the men out there woman is not written in braille. You don t have to touch her to know her. In fact the perspectives and the ideologue that the nationalists have are of the continental in origin and immigrant in nature and practice.

The proposition of the paper is to analyze the issue of Rape from socio-cultural point of view. It also deals why and how the understanding the concept of *Rape* is different from Indian feminists point of view to that of Dalit and subaltern feminists with reference to the select Dalit and Subaltern narratives.

Key words: Feminism, Rape, Dalit, Subaltern, Caste, Indian Feminism, Western Feminism, socio cultural aspect.

Introduction

Taking the issue of *Rape,* the India feminists statistically claim that according to the National Crime Records Bureau,

24,206 rape cases were registered in India in 2011. A new case is reported every 20 minutes, although the latest estimate suggests a new case every 22 minutes. In 2012, the conviction rate for rape was 24.2%. In fact they fail to study who are thewomen being raped and which caste do they belong to? They also fail to study the authentic reasons behind the issue of *Rape* whether it is due to biological or sociological differences.

The proposition of the paper is to analyze the issue of Rape from socio-cultural point of view. It also deals why and how in understanding the concept of *Rape* is different from Indian feminists point of view to that of Dalit and subaltern feminists.

Crime against women hit the newspaper, television, and social media networks daily. The reaction from the public reaches its momentum when the issue of rape hits the limelight and slowly it ebbs with the women going out for a march with candle light or voicing out against the crime in the social media network. Post the Nirubaiya incident has anything in the society change by taking effective steps or it has been nullified, it is as usual a heated debate. Whenever a girl is being molested or raped more than thousands of people discuss about it and more columns in the newspaper deal with it, more than million times it is being spoken by the politicians, journalist, celebrities, religious leaders and so on. Everyone has something to say about it and contribute their idea to it but what actually happens is that it never reaches the victim and no proper action is been taken through law to the affected girl. What happens to the rape victim after the rape is unknown to the public more than the rapist the girl raped is focused in the media and more debate takes place for the reason of the rape and in more case the girl is accused for her dress, or late night going out. Is the society accepting her, is she getting wedded to another person in spite of her being raped, how the family and neighbours of her treats her is not being addressed. There is much report being piled, files after files regarding the rape victims but in reality the humiliations, the torcher the pain suffering is not being addressed properly. Even though it is addressed the rapist is not given proper punishment under the law. The human rights commission involves in it and reduces the level of punishment.

The gender inequality is the main reason for rape in the society. Mostly the women who work in call centres and whose jobs are associated with the night shift and corporate field are the main victims. The rural women are being mostly affected due to their survival in the remote residential areas. Mostly children are being raped if the dress code that tempts the man to rape then why is old women and children being raped. In most of the rape cases the rapist is either a neighbour or a relative known to the victim.

In the early years the woman were considered to be the prey and property for man who are the natural predator. There was no safety for the women in the society and the burden to safe guard her was later formalised as husband, father, brother. A crime committed against her body became the crime against the male estate. In the beginning the male concept of ownership was forcible extension of his boundaries to his mate and later to their offspring. Susan Brownmiller gives the definition of rape as "If a woman chooses not to have intercourse with a specific man and the man choose to proceed against her will, that is the criminal act of rape" (18) later in the years according to ancient Babylonian and Mosaic law a payment of money like fifty pieces of silver was given to the father for the theft of virginity of the daughter.

In Hammurabi code the women were not given independent status as the female should either be betrothed girl living with the custody of her father or she should be a lawfully wedded wife living in the house of a husband. If a man rapes a betrothed virgin the girl is considered to be out of crime and the rapist was found guilty. If it is a married woman then she has to take the blame equally. The Hebrew punishment of rape was that if a girl was raped within the walls of the city then both shares the punishment of facing death through stoning. During the rule of King Athelstan in the tenth century the punishment was severe for rape "If a man were to throw a virgin to the ground against her will, "he forfeits the kings grace; if he shamelessly disrobes her and places himself upon her, he incurs the loss of all his possession; and if he lies with her, he incurs the loss of his life and members" (25). The vengeance continued and the punishment not only affected him but even the things associated with him like "even his horse shall to his ignomy be put to shame upon its scrotum and tail, which shall be cut off as close as possible to the buttocks. A similar fate awaited the rapist dog, and if he happened to own a hawk, let it lose its beak, its claws and its tail" (25). During the reign of William the conqueror the castration and blinding was the punishment as stated "Let him lose his eyes which gave him sight of the virgin's beauty for which he coveted her. And let him lose as well as the testicles which excited his hot lust" (25)

Feminist and Feminism started to get into the stream as the people saw feminism as the war between the sexes than the political struggle to end a sexiest oppression. The reasons behind the war between the sexes are due to the sexual discrimination, exploitation and oppression. The battle ground is always home as a proverb of Bantu speaking Gusiis of south west Kenya goes as "Those whom we marry are those whom we fight" (17). Bell hooks opines that feminism can end the war between the sexes as "it can transform the relationships so that the alienation, compensation and de-humanisationthat characterize human interaction can be replaced with feeling of intimacy, mutuality and camaraderie" (35). Eradicating the sexiest oppression will bring equality in the society as it is the basic of all other oppressions. Racism and class oppression is also stemming from the sexist oppression. Sexiest oppression is of primary importance not because it is the only oppression but it is the practice of domination that most people experience they may play a role of discriminator or discriminated against, exploiter or exploited. Though the sexist oppression cannot eradicate or eliminate all other forms of oppression it can make the other oppression intact as all the oppressions are connected to the social structure.

Bell Hooks says that "feminism is one radical political movement that focuses on transforming family relationships" (39). She further adds that feminism as a movement ends the sexiest oppression to bring a social change that will strengthen and sustain the family life in the entire household. Bell hooks conclude in her essay on *Feminist theory form Margin to Center* as "The fight against sexist oppression is of grave political significance- it is not of women only. Feminist movement is vital both in its power to liberate us form the terrible bonds of sexist oppression and its potential to radicalize and renew other liberation struggles" (42)

The society still expects the men to earn money and women to take care of the household. During the year 1963 Betty Friedans *FeminineMystique* was released and the book was given for fifteen prints during thecontinuous years. The book made the women think beyond the household. As the women rather than being a happy homemaker, contented wife and happy mother the women felt that they were intellectually and emotionally oppressed stopped by the limited options which the society left open to her. Their mystique stops with the identity of Mary's mom and tom's wife they don't want to have an individual identity. Most of the mothers insisted them not to be mere housewife like them even though the girl could not see beyond twenty two and they were engaged and married and led the life as their mother. Betty Frieden brings out the anguish of six years old mother as "Wish Id studied more sciencc, history, government, gone deeper into philosophy... Wish Id develop a deeper and more creative life of my own and that I hadn't become engaged and married at nineteen. Having expected the ideal in marriage, including a hundred per cent devoted husband, it was a shock to find this isn't the way it is" (68) The term masculine and feminine are used only in legal papers and forms but in reality they are like the two electrical poles. Simon de Beauvoir states that man is right in being man and it is woman who is in the wrong. Women are always seen in terms of body, as women have ovaries and uterus and these things imprison her in her subjectivity. Women is often termed that she thinks with her glands. Men ignore the fact that they also have anatomy as they include testicles and they secrete hormones. Women are always seen as an object of sex as anatomy is women's destiny. The identification of a woman is determined by her biology. Betty Friedan says that women have to shed her immaturity that has been called feminity in order to get the full human identity. This crisis of identity was there hundred years ago and in order to overcome the identity the women have to suffer to become fully human.

Women are always compared to the moon and water and men are compared to the sun and air as in the Hindu sacred marriage the man says "I am sky and you are earth and she says I am earth and you are sky". In Masculine Mystique written by Andrew kimbrell draws the survey of the He and She characteristics as He- more self-oriented, very competitive, needs less intimacy, more independent, strong drive for power and money, more sex-oriented, more aggressive, more manipulative and more polygamous. The she list are- more other focused, less competitive, need more intimacy, more dependent, power and money are less important, less aggressive, less manipulative and more monogamous.

Draupadi is written in Bengali by Mahasweta Devi and translated in English by Gayatri Spivak. It deals with the condition of women of lower class. The setting of the story is Naxal Bari movement. Mahaswetha's short story Draupadi reveals a story of a 27year old woman who is punished in sexual violence by the army officials.

There are much similarity between the Vyasa's Draupadi and Mahaswetha s Draupadi. First one is 'Disrobing of Draupadi in vyasas masterpiece Mahabharata, Draupadi gets her robe miraculously whereas Mahaswethas Draupadi refuses to be clothed in order to make the insurgence feel guilt of their act. In the both characters there is a 'power within' in the most crucial moments of their lives. In the morning she walks to the general naked and says "you asked them to make me up; dont you want to see how they made me?" The way Draupadi tears her piece of cloth with her teeth and the way she walks towards him in the bright sunlight with her head high and the state of her condition freezes the general. The officers believe that this is a form of punishment will weaken her but they are easily succeed in only stripping her but her empowerment after so much struggles slaps the officials of their third degree punishment in sexual violence. Draupadi stands for whole tribal women who are in the same condition.

The Indian politicians on the issue about rape are horrifying Mr Patil home minister of Madhya Pradesh says that even if we provide one policeman per house we can't stop crimes against women... The rise and atrocities against women is due to obscene images used in advertisements. Mr Gaur home minister of Chhattisgarh said on 5 June. It [rape] is a social crime which depends on the man and the woman. It is sometimes right and sometimes wrong. Mulayam Singh Yadav puts forth that such incidents [rapes] do not happen deliberately. These kinds of incidents happen accidentally he further added that boys make mistakes. They should not be hanged for this. We will revoke the anti-rape laws. Dharamveer Goyat senior politician in Harayana state reports that if the limit of morality is crossed by women, such cases will happen, he further adds that I have no hesitation in saying that about 90% of the girls consensually go with men and then they end up meeting criminal minds and become targets of rape.

In most of the cases the Dalits in the rural areas are being raped and most of them are not registered and if registered they are not taken serious steps to prevent these issue. The sufferer's fate is not known to the media or public but the issue of rape hits the media if it takes place in capitals or metropolitan cities. How many women who are raped come out with the same sprit into the public like Draupadi. Some lose their life when they are raped and post rape when they are in medication some die and the rest of the survivors hold on to the pain and struggles all through their life. Only few strong women try to come out and speak out about the abuses. If women assertion has to take place the equality between the genders has to be achieved and men has to be brought up in society in such a way to respect women and not to see them as a sexual object. Women should also try to voice out and the law in the country has to be strict to stop the issue of rape by giving them hard core punishment.

Reference

1. Beauvoir, Simone De. "Simone De Beauvoir The Second Sex, Woman as Other 1949." *Simone De Beauvoir The Second Sex, Woman as Other 1949.* N.p., n.d. Web. 12 Sept. 2016.
2. Brownmiller Susan, "*Against our Will: Men Women and Rape*", New York: Ballantine Books: 1975. Print.
3. Friedan Betty, "*Feminine Mystique*", Newyork: W.W.Norton: 1963. Print.
4. Gayatri Chakravorty Spivak Critical Inquiry, Vol. 8, No. 2, Writing and Sexual Difference. (winter, 1981), pp. 381-402.
5. Kimbrell Andrew. "*The Masculine Mystique: The Politics of Masculinity*: New York: Ballantine Books: 1995. Print.
6. http://www.bbc.com/news/world-asia-india-27808722

Chapter - IV

The Narratives of Sex and Religion: A Critical Study of Kancha Ilaiah's Untouchable God

A narrative is a report of the events presented to the readers in their local idiom by a narrator who may be the one who directly involved, witnessed or informed about something which he/she narrates. The narrator mainly deals with the effect or the result of an event and how the event he narrates has brought a great change in the society. The proposition of the present paper is to deal with the elements of sex and religious superiority with reference to Kancha Ilaiahs Untouchable God. As a part of the paper the realistic narratives (Dalit fiction) has been selected. The select narrative portrays the realistic facts by depicting sex, violence, caste discrimination which paved the way for the exclusion of the women in general and the Dalit women in particular. The select narrative is of high importance in dealing with the social evils like caste discrimination, gender violence the Dalit woman are subjected to experience not only by Caste-Hindus but also by their men.

Key words: narratives, sex, religion and caste discrimination.

In Untouchable God (2013) by Kancha Ilaiah the author depicts the reality of the women. The women of the upper caste and lower caste are treated as sexual dolls and concubines by men. They simply use them and throw away. Though the women who belong to lower caste are called untouchable but their body is touchable and they can be used as the men wish. In this novel Namboodri a Brahmin from Kerala who is twenty he goes to Govinda Nairs house and proposed his wish for mating his daughter Sita Mahalaxmi. With this happy news Govinda Nair went to tell his wife but his wife was weeping and said "My hopes arecrumbled. Do you really wish her to live in sambandham? With all the namelessness my life is better: she will have neither face, nor name. She will be the mother of Brahmin children but shall remain an unwed Nair. Can her children become Brahmins, let alone Namboodris? Can they become priests in any temple? You foolish man, how could you agree?" (28). She disagree to give to Brahmins but Govindan Nair roared "A Brahmin-Namboodri- is a God of Gods on Earth. Whatever they ask, they ask only to increase our virtue. Our Gods said that whatever a Brahmin asks, you must give it-whether it is wealth, cattle or daughter." (29) Govindan Nair said that as a spiritual demand he will give his daughter only to Namboodris and no one can stop it. Sita overheard the conversation and started weeping. By spending time around her mother she has learnt a lot about the world of women. But that world had no status of its own.

The day came where he and Sita were alone in the room and it was their first night. He experimented all the sixty four arts and it continued for many days and he said this is what Rama did to Sita and Vishnu did to Laxmi. She was forced to sleep with the Namboodri. She begot three kids for him. Aryavartha was the only country where the Gods exalted the spiritual sex. He was reminded of the Rig veda which contained slokas after slokas about how Indra, the God of Gods have loved women-not his wife of course- the apsaras, divine prostitute created by Gods to satisfy their own pleasure. He asked her how do you like this life Sita? She replied "I live the life of a dog, shut in a kennel, whelping every so often. When my master caresses me, I fawn on him," (39). While the Brahmin justified whatever they did was right either it be food, women, work or sex. "A Brahmin enters into the sexual act not for the appetitites of his physical body but for the pleasure of God, while the Shudras, the untouchables, the tribals- the undivine archaic people- enter into the act only to have their own selfish bodily pleasure." (30) So they were not considered to be divine. Hence the sons born to those castes do not have the power to send the fathers soul to heaven. This was the reason why they remained Shudras, Chandalas and tribals. "Occasionally he regretted that he had to perform his researches with such low material." (35)

On the other hand Namboodris sister-in-law Shiva Shakthi who was sitting on the verandah saw Namboodri coming she ran into the home like a rat that saw the snake gliding into the rat hole. She was a permanent widow her head was shaven and she weared mundu and her breast was covered with white pallu. Her days went in doing laboring in kitchen with wet clothes. Her relatives and other widows told her that she must not feel happy and free when she is alone but she really felt free in the absence of her dreadful brother-in-law. Namboodris elder brother died two years ago he believed in sati, though it was not under practice he couldnt do anything. He felt that

> "She must surely have been looking at men coming and going on the road. Hah! If I die, she will fly into the world of sex and romance like a bird with ten wings. Dont I know how these women are inside, never mind their fasts and mumbling? And then my brother will cast down from heaven. No chaste wife ought to be alive after the death of her husband: it only means shes secretly waiting for life to give her a chance at debauchery. Why else live? Better to enter the fire and purify the soul." (25)

When Isaiah an American black, who knows all about race journeys to India to know about the non- violence movement but he comes in contact with the Dalit people and discovers much else beside. Isaiah came to Benares he asks Jacob who are those women with white sari and their heads cleanly shaved. Jacob says "They are widows, they come here to live. They have nowhere else to go. Their families sent them here." (232) Only the upper caste widows were burnt on pyres, because upper caste men feared they might pollute the family's bloodline. Women cannot become Brahmins? The scriptures regard them as Shudras, unclean. Bankim Chandra called widowhood a "Vishbriksha a tree of poison." (238) Isaiah meets Mala she does research over there and she explains to him about the women she says that all the girls are widow. Some of them look no older than ten. In spite of the law the people will marry off their girls very young some time too much older men, they become widows inevitably and then they are packed off on pilgrimage to Varanasi or Kashi from which they are not indented to return. The lower caste women were treated as concubine they were made to clean the temple and they were forced to sleep with the temple priest. "No doubt that the men who control the ashrams feel like kings with enormous harems to boss around. They count their wealth in womens bodies. This is not as extreme or perverted as you might think: women have been an item of exchange for centuries." (240).

When Isaiah asked his doubt about their semi-naked status Mala uttered that they are like Gandhi. For which Jacob said "There was a mancalled Manu many centuries ago, who wrote a book saying that lower-caste women should always offer themselves to the gaze of the upper-caste men. If they cover themselves, they will be assaulted and punished." (183) He further said that Manu also said that Dalit should not own property, gold or ornament. They have to cook only in broken pot and eat in mutilated bowls. Elumalai narrated how the upper caste men made use of the lower caste women while saying his eyes became red "not from drinking liquor but from drinking history... the history of untouchable slavery...the history of womens untouchable bodies and touchable private parts." (192). The above mentioned facts reveals that how a women is being treated in India by the upper caste men and by the men of their own community.

II

Each religious people considered themselves as superior and the others as inferior and because of these concepts they separated the people and enmity was formed and it lead to the extent of murdering the people. In Untouchable God, Kancha Ilaiah represents the religious views of Brahmin through remarkable Brahmins of India. Veda Shastry of Tamil Nadu (where purest examples of exalted brahminhood are to be found) is the rightful leader. Namboodri of Kerala is from a caste that created the most perfect system of discrimination that the world has seen; Krishnamurthy of Karnataka and Appa Rao of Andhra Pradesh are slightly moderate; Tilak of Maharashtra dreams of increasing discrimination while Banerjee of Bengal believes he is above caste. The Brahmins lived in the other side of the village, far from Dalit Street. They lived in their divine feudal lands called agraharas. "The Gods gave those lands so they could stay away from the productive humans, socially connecting dogs and beasts of burden called donkeys." (5-6) The Hindu Gods has not stooped to create Chandalas, Paraiahs or dogs therefore the Brahmins hated them most. Paraiah felt the pain in him for being untouchable

> "Why then had the Gods allowed him to be born? If the Gods had nothing to do with it, maybe there were other Gods, enemies of the High Gods and creators of the fallen. But if so, where were these others? Why werent they doing their jobs? The High Gods gave their followers land, grain, money and status. If Paraiahs life was the gift of the other Gods, he would have liked to be able, just one, to tell them what he thought of them." (7-8)

When Namboodri on his way in the bus he saw people wearing shirts and he felt that during his days people were semi- naked. In this countrywere humidity and heat is prevailed it is good to see people half dressed and he felt that when he was a child in 1880s men and women wore only mundu. Kerala women never wore blouses. Prophet

Mohammed said to Arabs to come to Allahs mosque only with fully covered bodies wearing switched clothes from toe to head. Women wearing switched burkhas had come to spoil the women of Kerala. He felt that wearing clothes could be the end of all modesty. And when the Christian hospital people were giving treatment to the Paraiyar the upper caste people hated them and spoke ill of their religion. He was distracted by the man who sat beside him and some of his parts touched Namboodri. He felt that "Evil days: A Brahmin gets touched so casually by an unknown, perhaps an untouchable! These buses are profane places" (23) But the person was dressed well if he was an untouchable he would be smelt fishy and meaty so Namboodri asked his name he said Matthew, Namboodri snuffed "A Christian! This bloody Matthew could be of any caste! The Christians and Muslims in Kerala would definitely go to hell for spoiling the sanctity of Gods own country" (23).

British were spreading Christianity. Kerala is going Christian, going Christian was the household refrain of Brahmin families. In Kerala the Ezhavas who were toddy tappers, were revolting under the leadership of Narayana Guru. Namboodri called for the Meeting of the temple there were eight members and a British official. He saw the British officer chair and said this chair of Christian has to be removed. He ordered to remove the chair of the British beef eating Christian. Namboodri said "British had not only brought bad administration but also a bad God, a God who did not distinguish between Brahmin and Chandala. Even if they left tomorrow this Untouchable God would stay on here to spoil the air and water of Aryavarta." (48) Namboodri started running toward the church and he went inside and he saw the Jesus statue and he saw the priest speaking to the people of what God has told but Namboodri felt how can a God speak in prose to people directly, his mind was in whirl. He wants to live as a Christian, Namboodri said to his Sister-in-law. "But I do not wish to be, I cannot be, a Christian among untouchables. I cannot imagine that God is untouchable too. Can you find out if there is a Brahmin Christian anywhere in this Gods own country or outside it?" (53)

Caste conflict in the Syrian Church: Bishop Benjamin Chako refuses to Admit untouchables all such news in the paper instigated the religious riots in the city. The Bishop said I stand for the purity of Jesus, protecting Varnadharma and I will never allow the untouchables into the Churches. Hussein and Saraswathi studied together in the school and love blossomedbetween them. Their parents accepted and nikah was arranged Saraswati was changed to Mumtaj Bee and she went to her in-laws house. "A mosque education was followed by a mosque marriage and a mosque name. And a Hindu Saraswathi became a Muslim Mumtaj Bee." (78) It was Friday and people gathered for mosque but they saw Hussiens body in a pool of blood one eye socket empty and his private parts was cut and his chest was crushed and there was a note *"Any Cutorgan Dares To Marry A Hindu Girl ThisWill Be The Fait" (78).* Balarams house was so silent and outside the househung a banner *"If Mumtaj Bee Do Not Become Saraswati Within WeekShe Also Follow Her Husband"* (78). Under this someone has scribbled"*Any Shudra learns letter any were in world will have punishment likeSarwathi call Mumtaj Bee met.*"(78). The news of the murder was spreadin the newspaper. Many people gathered near the mosque to meet the chairman Yusuf Ali Khan. They discussed about the murder and they asked to type a pamphlet about the incident and they asked the people to distribute it after the mosque and then they can take the sword and cut as many head as possible but women should not be raped. The Muslim were planning to kill many more people."*Head For Heads...Two Heads For One PrivateOrgan."* (84)

Balaram saw a priest sitting in the temple, teaching four children. He approached the priest and asked for his daughter's education and the priest asked him which caste he belonged to and when he said he was Shudra the priest said

> "I am a pundit and priest of this temple. Above all I am a Brahmin. Do you think we teach Shudras, Chandalas, dogs and donkeys? Who let you march into the temple like this and ask me whether I would teach you low-born daughter-a girl, a damned bitch puppy! Get out! Out of this temple! Take your defiling feet off my floor!" (69).

The nine days of Ganesh was brought into the street. The Shudras distributed the Pamphlet. Some Paraiah came running to see the deity. Shudras stopped them and said "Dont come in here, you Paraiah Ganesh is a Hindu God. Not an Untouchable God." (97). Tilak came with his followers and said Ganesh will visit the Shudra street too. The Paraiah men shouted "We too have bodies. Are they not created by Gods? When the sound of our drums is touchable for God why not our bodies?" (97). After the festival Tilak invited all the people and told the tolerance behind the plan he told them briefly that one of the Brahmin is being arrested by the police and the Muslims are high in number we have to stimulate the lower caste Shudras and tell them that the Muslim men attacked their men in the market placeand if the rivalry between them broke out our Brahmin would be released and the investigation will turn upon the Shudras. He asked the people to heat the Shudras with passion and righteousness. "No Brahmin boy should go to jail."(91) The dressing sense of the Christian their food habits were being made fun off. Each religion considers itself to be superior and it people behaved like animal when it came to religious patriotism.

Conclusion

The caste discrimination inherited by birth leaves Dalits to face multiple oppressions that violate their economic, political, social and cultural rights. Being the most deprived section of the society they are the poorest, illiterate and easy targets for sexual harassment. The Dalits face not just caste violence inflicted on them by the dominant castes, but also gender and religious dominance. Education can only give them right to prosper and overcome the struggles imposed on them by the Caste Hindus. Learning will transform them and make them refined in terms of knowledge, improve their style of living and it will give them a critical thinking to question the atrocities done to them by the upper caste people in terms of gender, caste, religion etc.

Reference

1. Culler Jonathan, Literary Theory; A Very Short Introduction. New York: Oxford University press. 1997. Print.
2. <https://mrspolandssite.wikispaces.com/.../Kinds+of+Narratives+List-1pg> Ilaiah, Kancha, Untouchable God. *Kolkata: Samya,* 2013.Print.

Chapter - V

Dalit Assertion through Effective Characters: A Study of Joseph Macwan's Novel Stepchild

Angaliyat focuses mainly on the Vankar community, a Dalit communityin Gujarat, but the narrative develops around the structure of domination where the Patidar calls all the shots. The novel opens with two hardworking and simple Vankar friends who, motivated by a deep sense of dignity, confront Patidar youth when they make advances to a Vankar girl in the neighboring village. The incident is followed by a series of conflicts with the dominant community and ultimately both friends sacrifice their lives. It's not only their families, but the entire Vankar vas gets involved in this high drama, pain and suffering. Macwans narrative skills are both engaging and complex, sharply pointing out the enemy, within and without. The preposition of the paper will deal with the effective characters portrayed in the novel.

Key words: Dalits, Stepchild, Community, conflict.

Setting

The setting of the novel takes place in three different districts namely Shilapur, Kedaria and Ratnapur. Shilapur is the place where the vankarvas friend Valji and Teeho are living their main occupation is weaving and later they go for auction to the nearby place Ratnapur. Ratnapur is the place where the Patels dominate the Vankarvas and when Valji and Teeho go for auction they come across the patel making fun of the vankar girl and then Teeho takes the lead and then on the vengance, hatred and bloodshed stars between the Vankarvas and Patels. Kedaria is the place where the childhood husband of Methi resides. When the conflicts comes between the patels and vankavas then the patels secretly plan for seducing Methi and they end up in instigating bad thoughts in the mind of her childhood husband Chuntia. Finally things settle but the enimity between the castes never ends.

Time

The narrative style of Macwan moves on a linear progression as he never goes back to flashbacks and he never has spiral movement. Opening of the novel discusses about the relationship and the bonding between the characters and how they are connected internally with love. Later on it moves to various other incidents which make the reader get to know the discrimination, vengeance, hatred in the name of caste.

Characters

Teeho

Teeho is the main character in this novel he is a man who sticks on to his own beliefs and tradition he never blindly follows any ritual. He was eighteen when his parents had died one after the other in a matter of a year. He had fed the pallbearers when his father died but when it came to his mother s death he turned his face away at the mention of the twelfth day. While the other fellowmen felt that he was greedy for his father's money. For which he said "you will merely eat and forget. How will it benefit my poor dead parents? I dont see how your eating and drinking can reach my wretched parents! The good deeds they earned are gone with them; the rest is only display and Im not for it. You people may do what you like" (3). Teeho and Valji were close friends though Teeho was younger to Valji, much bigger built, but not yet married; and all schemes and efforts at getting him to marry had been aborative. He was an enterprising business man, very skillful and thrifty. He has inherited three houses and a productive ancestral loom. With all this he never had any bad habit. Teeho and Valji are good friends they fight whole night but it never alters the love between them. "If one were to seem them in that state, one would have thought that they never saw eye to eye. But these two were an unusual pair. Inseparable, two bodies with a single soul."(2) Only two person in the village can engage Teeha in plain speaking they are Valo and other is Bhavaankaka. It was world war time and the cotton was sold under control but Teehos involvement in cloth making made auction very profitable and in fact he would help the poor people with clothes and they would pay off the debut on time. It was the time when a bull sprang into the bazaar and it heeded straight to the clothes of Teeho but brave Teeho caught hold of the bulls hump and brought it to subdue to him and from then on he was considered to be a brave men in the village. He would sell his auction for 500-600 rupees but still he was not robbed by the highway man even when he returned home late night. When a stone was casted on the pot which a girl carriedand when she was drenched in water Teeho questioned the man who did such unjust thing. Even after knowing that it was uppercaste men he was dare enough to pick up fight with them and he attacked the troublemaker and his companions and he was brought to the village square at that time he withdrew the sword and told mukhi " Thakore, it is your responsibility to ensure that this bundle reaches me. Any true son of his mother may come forward. This "bhavani sword knows no friends today" (27). He holded high values in living he never married after the murder of his beloved friend Valji. When Kanku asks Teeho to give acceptance to Methis marriage he says

> "Teeho has taken an oath bhabhi, if you have denied yourself the world in your widowhood; I have denied myself my desires in the separation from my friend. Youve become a widow in a worldly sense, I have become a widower in another. Not Methi alone, but that very direction has become inimical to my existence. Bring that up again over my dead body" (118).

He gives shelter for Methi and her son and takes care of his education and till the end he serves the people and due to Methis urge he marries vali and makes a life of his own with two boy babies but still he takes care of Methi and her son and looks after the marriage of Methis son. One day when he goes for auction to the town with his son there he is being attacked by the upper caste men and beaten to death.

Valji

Valji is three years older to Teeho he is close friend of Teeho and he will go to the extent to risk is life for him. He is married to Kanku and has one son he tells that "I owe so much happiness to you Teeha!" (2). Kanku proved to be a best better half for Valji she supported him a lot. Valji understood his wife that "she wasnt just his wife, but his true companion. Very practical, extremely affectionate and truly committed to his happiness. On the whole, she was more concerned about others, rather than herself"(4). She mourned a lot for his death. He risked his life to make Teeha get married to Methi. Valjis mother Monghi was the second wife of Bijal. After few days of marriage to someone else Monghi went back to her parents and been divorced. Bijal had falled in love with Monghi and a month after the divorce of her they were married. Valji was born in the seventh month. But people took it in a wrong way saying that Valji was not the son of Bijal. They said that" Valo is not Bijals child; he is from the previous house. He was born here, that's all. Otherwise he is definitely an angaliyat" (68). These words made Bijal angry and he sent word to the Brahmin and to all mohalla to have meal in their household and he stated that "Those who considerValji as his son may come; the rest who think he is an angaliayat can stay away!" (68). Everyone came home and had the meal though they had diverse opinion towards the child they kept calm and never talked about it. Valji was lost in thought Dana asked Valji to have the food but he told him that he was disturbed by his wifes words. He further said that "I can't get these damn thorns out of my flesh- how long will the world consider me an outsider?" (69).

One day he put forth the proposal of marriage to Teeho but he never accepted it and it lead to fight between them and Valji promised that he would not step into his threshold nor see his face again but the next day morning as soon as the rooster crew valji went towards Teehos house such was the friendship between them. Bhavankaka helped them and gave moral support to them always he was the man behind them in taking decisions for their life. When he ran after the car to rescue Methi he was attacked badly and he fell from the car "with blood-filled eyes he had momentary and fading vision of Kanku smiling with a son in her arms, Teeha breathlessly slapping the loom and that was the end of his consciousness. The arms that reached out to hold his son collapsed lifeless on the sand" (77). Valji was Teehas soul without him Teeha was like a body without soul, an unlighted lamp.

Bhavaankaka

Bhavaankaka has inherited from his forefathers a natural intuitiveness and foresight. People looked up to him for his knowledge wisdom, and presence of mind that he brought to bear upon intricate problems. He knew how to separate the grain from the chaff. That's why it was said even among the upper caste that "there was none like Bhavaankaka within hundred miles" (52). It was only through a quirk of fate that a person like Bhavaankaka was born in an inferior caste like Vankars. After the death of Bhali his wife he bade goodbye to the worldly and personal matters. At the age of 26 he lost his family. It has been seven decades and six years but he has no desire left over. He was a great support to Teeho and Valji. It was for Teehos marriage he went to Heera to talk about the wedding between Methi and Teeho. When he came to know that Teeho was beaten to death by the upper caste men he lost hope and was broken and he left the village and no one knew where he went. All through his life he lived with great values and his philosophy helped other people.

Methi

Methi was a Shilapaar girl. She met Teeha when he fought for her with the uppercaste men. She developed love on him. Even though they belongedto different Paragna they planned to get married and she told Bhavaankaka "There is very little traffic between our villages. I may not be able to send a message again; on the noon of the next full moon day, I shall be waiting for him, like Okha, here by the fallow land. Hire a van, if need be, and rescue me!" (57). But when the tick was played by the upper caste patels towards her she felt broken and it ruined her life. When she knew that Valji died in terms of rescuing her she felt the pieces of jigsaw fell into place, her heart splintered. "Valji was Teehas soul. Without him Teeho was like a body without a soul, an unlighted lamp. He had died because of Methi. How was she to show her face to Teeha? Would he accept her.

Teeha is not interested in marrying at all after losing his best friend? There was a tragic clarity in Methis mind: "All avenues are closed to me now!" (80) With a scroaching sigh, she lamented valas death.

When she received the false letter of Teeho stating her to get married and settle in Keradia. She does according to his wish after long time of waiting to rejoin. In Chunthias house

Methi continued to live her life. She made the house clean and her clean behavior changed the bad qualities of her husband too. She gained reputage in the place. She even helped Khushlas daughter-in-law deliver a baby. She sent word to Moti and Ujjam that she was happy. When she went to her house everything was changed her husband came in the night fully drunk and he started beating Methi and abusing the child by saying it was not his child. It continued everyday Methi could not bear the humiliation and she went to Khushals house and his daughter-in-law explained the incident which happened in her absence. Everyday Chunthia attacked his wife brutally and for ten days he never returned to the house. Finally one day he arrived and started attacking the child now it was time for Methi to rebel back she also attacked her husband and knocked him down on the floor. She knew that she has murdered her husband. It was midnight she went to Khushals house and asked help from him to accompany to her parental house.

She felt to finish her life at that time she was saved by Teeho and brought home and she continued to live there. Later in the morning she came to know her husband was alive. She lived separately till she died. She persuaded Teeho to get married and start his life and she helped all the women who are pregnant to give safe birth. She proved to be a good midwife. Teehos loss hurted her so much and after some days she too passed away.

The effectiveness of the Dalit novel lies in the assertive characters which portray the sufferings and injustice upon the Dalits. Each characterin its own way opposes the upper caste society by rebelling against the atrocities. Finally some characters succeed in their attempt while other sacrifices their life for their own community people.

References

1. Feminist Theory: Examining Branches of feminism, N.p, n.d. Web. 21 Sept 2016 p. 1.

2. Macwan Joseph (2004). The Stepchild. Oxford University Press, New Delhi.
3. Suryakumari.A, "*Women Studies: An Emerging Discipline*", New Delhi: Gyan Publishing, 1993. Print. p. 8.

Chapter - VI

Narrating the Emergence of the Dalit Politics and Vengence: A Comparative Study of Joseph Macwan's Step Child and Sharankumar Limbale's Hindu

Dalit means untouchable in Chaturvarn. The transformation from past Dalit consciousness into its present condition is the birth spring source of Dalit literature. Being a Dalit and to possess Dalit consciousness are two different things. Literature that is created with Dalit consciousness about Dalit life is Dalit literature. The hardships of dalits are not simply due to their poverty, economic status or lack of education, but are a direct result of severe exploitation and suppression by the upper class, which is legitimized by Hindu religious scriptures.

The proposition of the present paper is to portray the experiences of the Dalits who were tensed and remained homeless due to the animosity of the Caste Hindus. The struggle for power is being depicted in this novel *Hindu* and how a Dalit suffers to become a leader and what are theconspiracies made behind it and how the upper class people dominate and oppress the lower caste people to get hold of power is narrated in this novel. Finally the author proves to the society that leaders are not born by birth they are made to become leaders by the people. As Lincoln stated that the rule of democracy is "For the people, of the people and by the people. Limbales *Hindu* depicts the struggle for power and Joseph Macwans *Stepchild (Angaliyat)* focuses mainly on the Vankar community. The novelopens with two hardworking and simple Vankar friends who, motivated by a deep sense of dignity, confront Patidar youth when they make advances to a Vankar girl in the neighbouring village. The incident is followed by a series of conflicts with the dominant community and ultimately both friends sacrifice their lives. Not only their families, but the entire Vankar vas getsinvolved in the high drama, pain and suffering. Both the novel shows the upper caste dominance and how the Dalits as a common people overcome the situation and win over the upper caste people is evident in these novels.

Key words: Oppression, Dominance, liberation, power and politics.

In Step child the caste discrimination is depicted clearly. The novel is about the community of weavers, the Vankars, is subject to oppression from the more powerful upper caste of the Patels. When Teeho and Valji went for auction in Shilapaar they come across the incident where an upper caste man caste a stone on the pot of charming young women, she was drenched and abashed and around her feet the broken pot was shattered. This humiliated Teeho who is a weaver from Ratnapur he went forward to question the patel men who casted the stone but the men and his companions said to him that "you mind your own business, outsider! The fellow raised his voice to snub Teeho" (16). But Teeho attacked the upper caste men and his companions. The trouble maker's companion got angry and came forward to attack Teeho "A low-caste man publicly humiliating an upper-caste, a patel no less! How could anyone allow this? "(16). Teeho grabbed him by the collar and threw him around. Valji took the measuring rod in his hand and waited to deal with other three fellows. The village mukhi arrived to the spot and he was aware of the situation and its happenings. Megho Patel told the mukhi that "You are the mukhi. I want to file a police complaint against this *dhed* (low-caste). The situation went out of control and the upper caste men started attacking

Teeho and he was wounded with blood stain. Teeho felt so bad that no one came forward to say "Teehabhai, you have saved us from disrepute" he understood that no one wanted to be on the wrong side of the patidars.

> "Teeho was aware of this in fact it filled him with contempt. The entire mohalla consisted of eighty houses. If all of them stood united, the twenty-five families of the patels would be powerless, but if they couldnt even dream of standing up for themselves, how were they to face the patels? The money was with the patels, Infact, as far as money was conserned, even the Thakore depended upon the Patels. In such circumstances to pick a fight with them was impractical and foolish" (18).

On the way Methi met him and invited him to his house it was for the girl whom he picked up the fight. In her home Moti her bother said that "But you know how it is- first of all our caste is a low one, and then one cant live in water and risk enmity with the crocodile" (19). While in thevillage square the upper caste men were in a rage "The Patels argued that if a low-caste man and an outsider at that, had publicly beaten up a Patels son, he must be taught a lesson for life" (26). In India it is under the pretext of the Caste and in the Western World it is under the name of the Race every exploitations takes place.

The Rivalry between the upper caste and the lower caste people leads to many problems. The enmity which started in Shilapaar when Teeho attacked the Patels it arose to many problems in and around the villages the Patels destroyed the land of Heera Khana and they hung a threatening note that

> "If you have anything to do with any of your community members in Ratnappar or let any of them enter here, that will be your end. You will be thrown out of the village, without even a drop of water from the lake. If you wish to live in this village harmoniously, then let Moti Dhula

> and Heera Khana be ostracized and made to answer for their conduct!" (29).

The Patels were agitated with the issue of Teeho attacking them and they wanted to take revenge on him so they were desperate to ruin Teehas life. The love which Methi and Teeho had developed were know to these people and they were waiting for good time to spoil it "She goes around like a sati, let her be saddled with this one, it will straighten her up for life. If Teeha has to live this knowledge, his life will be miserable. There is no punishment worse than this" (38). The evil intention of raping Methi underwent a change instead they planned to ruin her future. They called Methis child marriage husband Chunthia and they told him that

> "We have heard that Heera is not arranging the aanu and somebody from another paragna is making plans to elope with your wife. The caste may be yours, but our village will earn a bad reputation! This kind of thing had never happened before in any caste. We have not let it happen. And even now we don t want it to happen" (39).

For which Chunthia never agreed and said "You think I am a worm, dont you? Who asked you to take the responsibility of my aanu? I spit on your money...! His words infuriated Meghi, his nephew manji and his worthless son Nanio and Nanji said "Look at that! What arrogance for a bloody dhedh!" (40).

A sly farmer from Keradia gave those people a helping hand and he got a mean-looking wizened man with filthy thoughts murmuring some idea to them and they carried out the plan well to ruin Methi and Teehas wedding. When Valji planned to make a secret way to fix Methis weddinghe asked Dano to help for fixing the taxi to bring Methi in the night but when they approached Gola he never accepted for helping them even when they accepted to pay thrice the amount. Then Dano remembered the help which Dhelavala promised he will do when he caught him in the night with Ramlo he never spread about it to the villagers so Dhelavala said "Look Dana, you seem to be a useful person. Ask for my help when you are struck someday. I will not turn you down" (72). So he approached him but he too played a cunning role by giving a helping hand but he spread the message to Meghiji and the plan got collapsed and instead of Dano and Valji it was Manji and Nanji taking Methi to Keradia and when Valji tried to rescue her he was beaten to death. When Dano approached Heera to talk about Teehos acceptance for their daughters wedding the secret plan made by the upper caste people was revealed which ruined both Methi and Teehas future. Heera showed the letter written by Teeha to Methi stating her to get married and not to wait for him anymore but it was the plan of the patels and it was they who wrote secret letter to Methi. After this letter Methi got married to Chunthia and Teeho remained unmarried. Even after so many years once when Teeha went into the town for auction when Dano and Jeeva was not there he was beaten up to death. "Eight to ten young men came crushing down upon Teeha. With sticks and punches, they left Teeha half dead." (226).

The law supported the people who belonged to the lower caste. The upper caste people thought they can do anything with money and power but in this novel whoever does the crime are being punished while the law never works in favour of the caste, power, or people. When the upper caste people destroyed the fields of Heeras fields with the help of Master Valji and Teeho met the Collector and explained the whole incidents which took palce in Shilapaar. The next day police came to arrest the people who destroyed the field and asked Teeho to give the names of the people without fear of who attacked him and destroyed the fields of Heera. For which Teeho replied

> "To tell the truth Saheb, I am not at all afraid of anybody. Why should I be afraid when we have a government of people like you? If they cronfront me one at a time I would relish even dying in the process. It's so difficult to

cope up with the harassments of our people and conspiracies that take place behind our backs" (48).

When Valji was killed the police went to Keradia and rescued Methi and arrested the people who were behind the death of Valji.

"Manji, Nanji and Gola were found guilty on the charges of conspiracy and execution of the murder of Valji, and were sentenced for life. Dehlavala was made to serve internment for a month and ahalf and charged with a fine of 1000 rupees for playing an indirect role in the conspiracy. On the other hand, Meghji patel and Khushlo were given the benefit of doubt since there was no evidence of their direct and indirect involvement" (105).

When the riot between Jeevan and Dehlavalas car driver Ramlo broke out there was a huge rage in Ratnapaar. The people started attacking each other and they were searching for Jeevan with blood rage. Dano Jeevan and Teeho went to master and told about the whole situation. Master picked them to police station the DSP never responded properly to the situation since they were under Dehlavalas control. Master asked the driver to go to Ahmedabad the car reached Gandhiji's ashram. Master went and met Gandhiji's senior followers and told about the happenings in Ratnapaar and about Dehlavala. Within that day all arrangements were made and a letter from Regional President reached Dehlavala it stated that he should ask forgiveness to the vankarvas and later it will be reported whether he will be allowed to continue or dismiss the party. Before Master left he said to Dehlavala that" The sun of Gandhi Bapu is still warm in this country, Dehlavala "(201).

Though Goka was not his own son Teeho took care of him and the importance of education was given to him and after his death he made his name immortal through Goku. After few months Dehlavala had appeared as a respected minister to host a meeting for the plans to put up a high school. And it was announced that those who give five thousand and one rupee as donation the name of the donor will be placed in the marble plaque. Standing from a distance Goka spoke up: Rupees seven thousand and one from me, heads turned to him the man noting down asked in whose name, Goku proudly answered In the name of Teehabhai Gopalbhai Parmar!

The Caste discrimination in Hindu is depicted clearly through politics. This novel *Hindu* seeks to highlight the power politics and further consequences that lead to the killing of a Dalit youth, raping of a Dalit woman and further legal operations from both the caste Hindus and the Dalits. In this novel Hindu Kasbe tells that there is a talk about Prabhakar Kamble becoming the next patil, the head man of the village. As Rambhau Kamble the headman will retire in two years. Then "Tatya Kamble will get a chance as the post will be reserved for dalit candidates as by law" (4). But Rambhau Kavale will never step down the village headship which his family has enjoyed. He will make sure that his son becomes the next patil.

Miland seated in the car with Gopichand and Manikchand was on the way to enjoy the night. The car crossed Bhimnagar decorated with buntingsand banner. Suddenly the headlight of the car showed the agitated crowd and Murder shouted Manikchand. Tatya Kambles blood soaked body was twitching by the roadside get the car moving shouted Manikchand. And car speeded up to Rambhau Kavales house. Miland said to him that there has been a Murder. And asked where was his son Prabhakar? For which patil told that he has gone to Pune to visit his brother Madhukar. Then he said to Kavale that he saw him in the crowd. Kavales face turned pale. Behind him stood his eldest son Sudhakar making odd gestures. He was mentally retarded. But hiding his emotions Kavale called them to dine with him tonight because they were his guest. For which Miland got shocked his eyes filled with tears and thought of Tatya Kamble. He was like a lion. The killers have erased the identity of the village as Jalsakar

Tatya Kambles village forever. He felt that "This was an attempt to teach a lesson to ordinary dalits by killing a dalit. Who was respected for his talents and had made a name for himself. It was the disfigured face of social terrorism. Dalits have been murdered for thousands of years."(12).

Manikchand said that Tatya Kamble was murdered and who knows where his brother Sadananad Kamble might be so we came for nothing tonight he said. "Kavale has removed the thorn called Tatya Kamble. Now he can have his son anointed as patil" said Gopichand. (12). Then Miland felt that now the law is on the Dalit side and the person who murdered him will surely go to jail. But paying the money they will get bail said Manikchand. Then Miland asked himself many questions was he dead or alive? Is he an activist or not a man? How can he be quite for the murder of Tatya Kamble? The car entered the farmhouse. Sadananad Kamble came running to open the gate he works as a watchman. He was Tatya Kambles brother he was not aware of the murder. He felt like holding him and weeping on his shoulders. But Manikchand strictly said to him not to say it to Sadananad because when he comes to know about the murder he will run into the village and he too will be killed so Miland kept quite.

Miland told them to tell Sadananad about the murder for which they said "Miland, we dont know what we witnessed to this event. Remember the three monkeys of Gandhi."(16). Prabhakar Kavale came into the room with blood rage. And caught hold of Manikchand legs and asked him not to reveal that he saw him at the murder spot. And Manikchand told that he won't do it and Prabhakar Kavale drank the wine in the glass and ate the mutton and he said to them that for seventy generations of Tatya Kamble family lived off the scraps which they discharged. But he did not respect our charity. The words of Prabhakar Kavale struck Miland and said to himthat he will reveal about him to the police and get him handcuffed. For which they both fought with each other.

Miland felt that "Muslims dont kill dalits, nor do Christians. Buddhist does not commit atrocities on dalit, nor do Sikhs. Then why do Hindus torment dalits? Dont they accept the dalits are Hindu too? (27). Rohit Kamble the son of Tatya Kamble lit the pyre. Tatya Kamble body turned to ashes in a moment. There was a total silence.

The law being in favor of the people the police visited Kavales Bara and every one was nervous. Then constable Marathe asked Rambhau Kavale about Prabhakar but he told that he was in pune. And the police told them that he was caught and kept in the prison. And police confiscated the sword hidden in the Bara. Constable Marathe and Gautama Gangurde laid a clever trap and caught Jaganath Pandit at his farm for the first time people responsible for committing reckless atrocities against dalits were behind bars.

The dominance of the upper caste people in education is seen clearly in this novel. The school reopened Kasbe Guruji was teaching a lesson on Babasaheb Ambedkars. The news spread in the village, Narendra Patil and other people went into the school and they tore the pages of that book. Kasbe Guruji applied for transfer and felt that it was a castiest village and he felt unsafe there. And he asked to transfer him to another place. Soon the news reached villages. And they were also waiting for his transfer but God bole Guruji and Kasbe Guruji were engaged in a heated discussion that not all Hindus are castiest. Hindu religion is tolerant religion to. Then Kasbe told him that "you are right. We should consider the cow holy and the untouchable unholy. Offer milk to the poisonous snake and murder the untouchable. Is this what you call tolerance?"(36).

Even since Sonali came to Achalpur, as a new bride, she was enchanted by the sound of dholaki drums. She was married to Prabhakar and she heard the drums and went upstairs to see the dance. Her heart ached thinking of the sweet and sour memories of her happy college days. She was given a dance recital at the annual function and that gained a lot of fame for her and the local papers published her photographs and interviews and along her side in the paper there were Rohit (Tatya Kambles son) a dalit boy she even praised him and it created anger with the savarnas. She and Rohit got to know each other only in the dance and they became close friends. While the savarnas boys sent the photograph of Rohit and Sonali dance together to her father. As soon as Baliram Patil saw it he felt angry. Sonali had the habit of writing poems and many got published too and when Sonalis dairy of poems got into her fathers hand he mistook it and put an end to Sonalis education.

The rivalry between the upper caste and lower caste men in *Hindu* is depicted through politics. Madhukar Kavale was upset because he feared that Tatya Kamble would become the next patil. Vishnu Pujari felt that people were losing eternal faith as they were going to see jalsa and the collection of the money in the temple was becoming low and Jaganath Pandit felt that because of Tatya Kamble only he lost his job. All of them were unhappy with Tatya Kamble for one reason or other. Tatya Kamble gave speech about Ambedkar by quoting his words

> "Why do you stay in a religion that does not allow you to enter the temple? Why do you stay in a religion that does not acknowledge your Humanity? Why do you stay in a religion that does not allow you even water? A religion that forbids the treatment of human as human is not a religion but nacked domination. A religion in which touching of unclean animal is permitted but touching of human is prohibited is not a religion but insanity" (50, 51).

Sonali went upstairs to see the jalsa being performed. For first time she felt that speech was like erupting volcano.The people were waiting to murder Tatya Kamble at the village square. Prabhakar Kavale, Gunvant Patil,

Jagannath Pandit, Balshetwar were hiding and they came running out with weapons in their hands, and pounced upon Tatya Kamble. But somehow he got out of their clutches but Shankar Pujari grabbed him as he started to scream the village doors began to close one after the other, Prabhakar had a sword, Gunvant had a spear, Jagannath Pandit an axe and others had knife. Sonalis heart sank as she saw the massacre. At that precise moment Manikchand and Gopichand car arrived on the scene and the violent crowd dispersed. Tatya Kamble fell on the ground. Sonali froze and she walked down the stairs slowly. The crowd broke out and they were scattered in different places. Manikchand car came near the gate of Rambhau and told that he saw his son murdering Tatya Kamble. And they made a secret dealing not to reveal it to anyone.

Later on after series of incidents Manikchand, Gopichand and Sadananad went in the car and they reached Hema Pandits house and they spoke to the people over there and Manikchand tells them that Sadananad is our man and we are planning for him to contest in the Assembly election next time and we want your support. Sadananad Kamble got the minister post and Achalpur celebrated his victory. A grand pooja was performed in the temple. After some years many people were on their way to the city to hear the judgment. The court compound was crowded. The dalit activists were present in large number to hear the judgment. The law supported thevillagers and Kavales families were happily waiting to see Prabhakar Kavale. The parade was nearing the Bara. Prabhakar Kavale was puffed with pride. Sonali stood facing Prabhakar, performing arti. Suddenly people saw Prabhakar Kavales body fall on the ground. It was Kabir Kamble who rained his bullets at Prabhakar Kavale. And Prabhakar Kavale is dead. Miland dialed Sadanands number. Pandit Kanade picked up the phone. Miland told him that Prabhakar Kavales is finished. But to his surprise he told that the news was old and he asked him do you want to hear the new one. Then he told that Madhukar Kavale saw Manikchand before the court judgment and gave him five boxes. And he told that Sadananad is angry that Manikchand and Gopichand are misusing his name to line their pockets. Thus the rivalry ends in the novel by the common man murdering the upper caste men.

Reference

1. Limbale Sharankumar. Hindu. Kolkata: Samya. 2010. Print.
2. Macwan, Joseph. Step Child. New Delhi: Oxford. 2004. Print.
3. Nimbalkar Waman. Dalit literature:Nature and Role. Nagpur: Prabodhan Prakashan. 2006. Print.

Chapter – VII

Dalit Fiction Realistic Fiction: Critical Study

Narratives are the works that provide an account of connected events. Literary narratives can be viewed in many types including novels, dramas, fables, folk tales, short stories, poetry, etc. A Narrative is a story, whether told in prose or verse. It involves events, characters and what the characters say and do. Starting point for interpreting and writing about imaginative work is to analyze the elements of Narration. The narrator mainly deals with the effect or the result of an event and how the event he/she narrates has brought a great change in the society. There are different kinds of Narratives. Subject to their possible settings and the typical elements and the characters they have, the narratives are classified as: (1) Adventures (2) Fables (3) Fairy tales (4) Fantasy stories (5) Folktales (6) Mysteries (7) Myths (8) Personal narratives (9) Realistic stories (10) Science fiction stories. The proposed paper is going to deal about the realistic narratives in the Dalit fiction. How the men faced caste violence and how the women faced suffering under the upper caste men and by the men who belonged to their own community. It will also portray the social evil and domination of the men in the society against women. Unlike other literature Dalit literature deals with the real life experience experienced by the writer or by the people in the community. It portrays the real life suffering faced by the lower caste men and women in the form of religion, caste and gender and class.

Key words: Narratives, Dalit, caste violence, domination, inequality.

Introduction

In this paper I am going to portray the oppression faced by the men in terms of caste and sufferings faced by the women in terms of gender in the three Dalit fiction (i) *The Step Child* (2004) (ii) *Untouchable God (2011)* and (iii) *Vanmam Vendetta (2008)*. The main reason behind Dalit literature is to question the Indian mythology and to deconstruct the ideas of oppression, suppression, discrimination within the community. As Dalit dont have a personal life as their life is constrained with the community and anything affects them as a whole they voice out for their well being. The Dalit men face the domination of the male from the upper caste and they act as a slave to them and Dalit women face the domination and inequality from the upper caste men and from the men from their own community as women and as Dalit women. In the three novels which are stated above have the similarity in terms of caste violence and gender discrimination and the characters in the novel face a fatal death due to the caste violence and it leads to series of problem resulting a drift in the harmonic life of the lower caste people. The worst inequality is being faced by the Dalit women. Women as a whole is considered to be inferior but Dalit women are more inferior and they face double discrimination from the men.

In the *Step child* (2004) Joseph Macwan portrays the caste violence faced by the lower caste men and how the protagonist questions the atrocities faced by the upper caste men and it leads to fatal murder even after many years. *Angaliyat (Step Child)* focuses mainly on the Vankar community but the narrative developes around the structure of domination where the Patidar calls all the shots. The novel opens with two hardworking and simple Vankar friends who, motivated by a deep sense of dignity, confront Patidar youth when they make advances to a Vankar girl in the neighbouring village. The incident is followed by a series of conflicts with the dominant community and ultimately both friends sacrifice their lives. It was not only their families, but the entire Vankar vas gets involved in the high drama, pain and suffering. Macwan s narrative skill are both engaging and complex, sharply pointing out the enemy within and without.

In *Vanmam Vendetta* (2008) the author Bama deals with the animosity between two castes within Dalits – Pallars (who identifies themselves as Hindus) and Parayars (mostly Christian converts). It also tells about the Naickers the land ownwers of the dominant caste stroke fire to preserve their status. Saminathans uncle Mariaraasu was tall and well built fellow he was the one who watered Ranga Naickers fields. The water from the irriagation channel has to be diverted to the various fields the landowners slept comfortably in their houses and it was the Pallars and Parayars who had to be outdoor in misty weather to water the fields at early dawn they was no one to care for them. Right to Ranga Naickers field was the one belonging to Palanivelu Naicker. The field was being watered by a Pallar named Karuppuswamy. "There were constant quarrels between Marraasu and Karuppuswamy about the irriagation water. Whereas Ranga Naicker and Palanivelu Naicker lived in peace, here the Pallars and the Parayars who were in charge of watering the respective field turned into sworn enemies." (Bama, 2004, p8) Ranga Naicker would instigate Marraasu and Palani Naicker would stir up Karuppuswamy. Without quarrelling not even a day would go between them. Palani Naicker went a step forward and told Karuppuswamy to be aggressive and promised to take care of everything.

One Sunday Marraasu left home to the fields that day it was the turn of Ranga Naickers field to get water. Marraasu reached the palce but Karuppuswamy had gone to divert the water to Palanivelus field. Marraasu noticed this and he dug a ditch to divert the water to Ranga Naickers fields. Karuppuswamy notice that suddenly the water got stopped. The quarrel broke up between them. Pichamurthy who had been working in the adjoining field heard the commotion and rushed there. He was a Pallar too he tried to stop the fight between them they both were not in a mood to listen. Marraasu asked Pichamurthy that it was his landlords turn to water the field but this fellow diverted the water to his land lord field. Pichamurthy said

> "Why did you divert the water out of the turn? Isnt that the reason for this unnecessary argument? Why all this fighting amongst us? Whether the fields are dry or watered, what is the gain to you? It's someone whos going to reap the benefit, but it's you two who are fighting! Let it go, both of you. Dont come and shout like this in the fields in the middle of the night. The very sound of it is un nerving" (Bama, 2008, p. 9).

Karuppuswamy told Pichamurthy that as soon as he came he just started diverting the water what does he think of himself is he a great lord? Then the fight got into physical commotion and they started to attack each other.

Marraasu was heft and he was drunk that day and he was not able to safeguard him. Karuppuswamy lifted the spade he was holding and he struck Marraasu hard blow on his head and he placed a stout stick on Marraasus throat and pressed it hard by his foot. Pichamurthy was pleading Karuppuswamy to leave him but he didn t listen and within a short while Marraasu lay dead. Saminathan was distressed whenever he thought of how his uncle marraasu has been murdered. His mother tells him that it was the coaching of the landlords that the Pallans are behaving so crazy.

"They are the ones who are plotting to make sure our two castes never unite. This has been going on for ten or twenty years now. In fact even in your forefathers time there had been this enmity. I dont know how many lifetimes it will take for our two castes to come together as friends. The way the things are going, it looks like it can never happen" (Bama, 2008, p. 12).

It was the uppercaste people who plotted against the peacefull life of the lower caste Pallar and Parayar

> "The Naickers became utterly scared. If the two castes were to work together and put up a common candidate, they could snatch away even the panchayat president post! They thought, all these years these people have been coming and standing before us with folded hands, ready to serve us; we mustnt get to a situation where we have to bow before them. And so the Naickers made plan to destroy the unity between Pallars and Parayars" (Bama, 2008, p. 15).

Marraasu was killed by a Pallan and how did Pallan do it was from the courage given by Palani Naicker. The Naickers tell the Pallars that "look, you and we are Hindus, and we Hindus must stick together" (Bama, 2008, p. 15). Chinnamma who worked in the Naickers field came to know about how the Pallars dance for the tune of the Naickers and said that "If a village is split into two, only the mischief-makers will celebrate." It's very true. Instead of being sensible and cooperating, the Pallans and Parayans are confronting one another with weapons drawn. Naturally the other caste people are only too delighted to stand by and watch" (Bama, 2008, p. 63).

In *Untouchable God* (2013) Kancha Ilaiah states the caste discrimination can be seen evident between the upper caste Brahmin and the other inferior caste. The Paraiah were the working class they have to work day and night without rest. They are squeezed till the last blood in their body. Paraiah had worked all day collecting the grains cut by women and bundling it so they could carry it away. Only an exceptional man like Paraiah did both male and female tasks.

"Yet in the life of Paraiah no pleasure seems to exist. All the really important things he did, like killing the chicken or bundling the corps, were for others, not for him or his children.

The only pleasure he tasted was that of feeding the corps with water and manure, and feeding his masters cattle. These acts marked him as a sinner, while his master, who owned both corps and cattle, but fed neither, was pure. The only truly pure thing, it seemed to him, was eating. The landlord ate for the benefit of the village, and the priest ate for the benefit of Gods." (Ilaiah, 2013, p. 4)

Paraiah felt sad because instead he suffered the endless pain that came when a human being was forced to lead the life of a dog. The Hindu Gods had failed to impress the divine separateness of caste on these dogs. The Brahmins lived in the other side of the village, far from this street. They lived in their divine feudal lands called agraharas. "The Gods gave those lands so they could stay away from the productive humans, socially connecting dogs and beasts of burden called donkeys." (Ilaiah, 2013, p 5-6)

The Hindu Gods has not stooped to create Chandalas, Paraiahs or dogs therefore the Brahmins hated them most. The Brahmins hated these things more than shit. The Brahmins felt that "God created the Brahmins from his head, the Kshatriyas from his shoulders, the Vaishyas from his thighs and the Shudras from his feet. The Panchamas-the filth-were unborn." (Ilaiah, 2013, p18) The Panchamas, of whom Paraiah was one, were never created by God.

Even in terms of education the upper caste men discriminated the lower caste people Balaram saw a priest sitting in the temple and teaching four children. He approached the priest and asked for his daughter's education and the priest asked him which caste he belonged to and when he said he was Shudra the priest said

> "I am a pundit and priest of this temple. Above all I am a Brahmin. Do you think we teach Shudras, Chandalas, dogs and donkeys? Who let you march into the temple like this and ask me whether I would teach you low-born daughter-a girl, a damned bitch puppy! Get out! Out of

this temple! Take your defiling feet off my floor!" (Ilaiah, 2013, p. 69).

Likewise the oppression faced by the lower men in caste discrimination and caste violence is being potrayed by the realistic narrative by the writer who belonged to their community. Likewise the women also faced oppression and inequality by the men.

In *The Step Child* Methi was a Shilapaar girl. She met Teeha when he fought for her with the upper caste men. She developed love on him. Eventhough they belonged to different Paragna they planned to get married. But when the tick was played by the upper caste patels towards her she felt broken and it ruined her life. When she knew that Valji died in terms of rescuing her she felt the pieces of jigsaw fell into place, her heart splintered. When she received the false letter of Teeho stating her to get married and settle in Keradia. In Chunthias house Methi continued to live her life. She made the house clean and her clean behavior changed the bad qualities of her husband too. After her delivery when she went to her house everything was changed her husband came in the night fully drunk and he started beating Methi and abusing the child by saying it was not his child. It continued everyday Methi could not bear the humiliation and she went to Khushals house and his daughter-in-law explained the incident which happened in her absence. Everyday Chunthia attacked his wife brutally and for ten days he never returned to the house. Finally one day he arrived and started attacking the child now it was time for Methi to rebel back she also attacked her husband and knocked him down on the floor. Althrough her life she faced suffering and humiliation and she could not get in unison with Teeho.

In *Untouchable God* men always considered them to be the superior and they considered the women to be of low birth and they were considered to be inferior. Several women were returning home after the long day s labour work. Harvesting the crops was mostly a female task.

"Men were men whatever caste they were born in; they tilled the land and fed the cattle but they would never cook, or weed crops. The division between the labour of men and women was so deep that it was almost a thing of nature; it was so old that no one could have said whether it was made by Gods or humans." (Ilaiah, 2013, p. 1)

In the priest Veda Shastrys house in the kitchen the women were wearing wet sari around their shivering bodies and cooking it gives satisfaction to Gods and they were preparing thirty three different dishes. The young women cutting the vegetable in the kitchen felt that "All the hours of the day we skulk in this rat hole of a kitchen, cooking nasty food that we will never eat. We can only know how our food taste from our mens praise or blame. I think Shudra women, Chandala women are better off than us." (Ilaiah, 2013, p. 12) Veda Shastry felt we must look for alternative arrangement for producing children. He said that there was once a king called Nala who was born in womens womb as his father coupled with another male. He said

> "If we could cultivate the habit of men mating with men, we could remove pollution from our lives forever. As it is we are constantly in peril from the filthy stink of women. They are liable to bleed at any time and destroy the sanctity of the sacrifice and the integrity of mediation; their wombs are poison cells." (Ilaiah, 2013, p. 15-16)

Appa Rao had a doubt that why do women cook in wet clothes? Our Gods enjoyed the food cooked by men in times past. For which Veda Shastry smile and said the same Nala who was born of a man was the finest cook in Aryavartha. He always cooked in wet clothes Even Bhima was an excellent cook thats why Nala and Bhima are always praised first. The food was being served and people ate the food Veda Shastry said "As we are inadequately manly we are forced to eat food prepared by spiritually polluted beings- women" (18). Even in the upper caste houses only the leftover food were eaten by the women. When Isaiah came to Dalit colony when they were having food only the men ate first when the women was asked to sit and dine "No, We women do not eat till all the men in the house have eaten" said Veeramma (Ilaiah 2013, p194). When Isaiah says that in our case men and women sit together and eat but and he said that "Our women eats more than we men eat". (Ilaiah, 2013, p195) Veeramma gives reply to Isaiah that "NO woman eats more than men. Men eat all the food and say we did not eat". (Ilaiah, 2013, p. 195)

When Isaiah saw semi –naked women on the roads he asked about it to Jacob and he explained "There was a man called Manu many centuries ago, who wrote a book saying that lower-caste women should always offer themselves to the gaze of the upper-caste men. If they cover themselves, they will be assaulted and punished." (Ilaiah, 2013, p183) Their Gods were different their Gods too did the same thing with our women and also men. Their Indra God was known for raping and keeping our women. Jacob and Isaiah went to book shop to purchase some book he took book on Rig Veda. He read some word in the book

> "God has made the caste: the Brahmins from his head, the Kshatriyas from his shoulders and arms, the Baniyas from his belly and the Shudras from his feet. The untouchables and women werent mentioned at all. He remembered the words of Genesis: "So God created man as his own image.In the image of God created He him, Male and Female created He them" (ilaiah, 2013, p. 212).

The women of the upper caste and lower caste are treated as sexual dolls and concubines by men. They simply use them and throw away. Thought the women who belong to lower caste are called untouchable but their body is touchable and they can be used as the men wish. Namboodri a Brahmin was twenty he went to Govinda Nairs house and he spoke to him and he proposed his wish for mating his daughter Sita Mahalaxmi and it was a forced acceptance by Sita as it was the Brahmin who put forth the views to get united without marriage she lead her life by satisfying the Brahmins lust.

In *Vanmam vendetta* the rift between the pallars and Parayars leads to the suffering of women in the village and they were being torchered by the police and they are left in their houses without the men. These women try to manage their food and lead their life without the help of their men. They voice out bravely for the murder that the Pallars did for the Parayars. In the prison the policemen kicked Chellakili in the lower belly with his boots and said "so you complained to the circle inspector about us, eh? Well rip up your mouth if you utter another word!"(pg86). Another policeman hit her hard on her lower back with his lathi. Chellakilli curled up and collapsed on the floor of the cell. "As she lay there on the floor of that police lock-up, she felt a sharp pain in her belly... And ...she had an abortion right there. She had lost her baby. What agony Chellakili suffered..." (Bama, 2008, p 86). After seven years she was carrying her baby but the policeman has kicked her and the baby. The women around Chellakili consoled her.

There were no men left in the Parayar Street only few women were there and they were determined to take the corpse of their men and clear it. Rosemary drove the cart and brought the corpse. "The women gathered together, took the bodies in the cart to the graveyard, dug a big grave all by themselves, and buried all three bodies in that single grave" (Bama, 2008, p87). The policemen were astonished to see the women doing the burial themselves. "these she- donkeys have so much guts, eh, they remarked" (Bama, 2008, p87) The next day policemen went into the Parayar street and started beating the women with lathis chasing them as they ran and raining blows on them, and cursing them in the foulest language. While the women were left all alone in the streets and they managed by milking the cow and distributing to other women and they were leading their life with the little food they had and they never went out for any work. Even to go to market they have to cross the pallar street. The upper caste people were basking in this issue of the lower caste. Slowly the life returned into normal. The men and women started living peacefully.

Thus to conclude the Dalit are being exploited physically, mentally and socially. They are treated very low and the upper caste people suck the blood of the lower caste people till the death. Though India claims freedom and states that it is the nation of equality and liberty but still the Dalit face the oppression and in order to overcome this poverty has to be eradicated and the future generation of the lower caste people must gain education to change the atrocities and humiliation faced by their own community under the pangs of the upper caste.

References

1. Bharti, C.B. (1999).The Aesthetics of Dalit literature.*Trans Darshana Trivedi Hyati.*
2. Bama., Malini Seshadri.(2008).Vanmam – Vendetta. *Delhi: Oxford.Print*
3. Ilaiah., Kancha.(2013). Untouchable God. *Kolkata: Samya, Print.*
4. Macwan., Joseph.(2004). Step Child. *Delhi: Oxford, Print.*

Chapter - VIII

Life Unsettled and Discrimination Unended: A Dalit Feminist Study of P. Sivakami's The Taming of Women

As a theory, feminism deals with the issues pertaining to the women and their identities in a society. The feminism, though the Western migrated, has its strong roots in India by questioning the way why and how Sita was sent out of the kingdom by her husband Rama in Ramayana and having Draupathi as a common wife for five brothers in Mahabaratha. There is certain ambiguity about understanding the feminism in Indian context like if Sita was a feminist, Rama would not dare to send her to the forest. Similarly if Mumtaj is a feminist, Sahajahan would not have built the Tajmahal. Hence the very definition of feminism in Indian context is a complicated debate especially when we apply the feminism so as to understand the life of the Dalits, Minorities and Tribal women. Hence the emergence of Dalit feminism does unmask the mask of Indian feminism claiming that the Indian feminism is exclusivist and religious oriented.

The Dalit feminism dares to interrogate the dominance of the Caste-Hindus of both men and women and challenging the imposed culture of silence over the dalits for centuries together by voicing their feelings, the Dalit women pave the way for reclaiming their esteemed culture and represent themselves through their narratives. The Dalit narratives especially by the Dalit women truly aim at representing the innate and unexplored experiences of the Dalit women in the male dominated Indian society. P. Sivakami *TheTaming of Women* (2012) is also one of such narratives that deal with the issues of caste and gender identities. The proposition of the paper is to study P. Sivakamis *The Taming of Women* which rightly offers us all possible critical and analytical means of life aspects of the Dalit women.

Key words: caste, gender, culture, orientalism.

Dr. C.B. Bharti claims: "The aim of Dalit Literature is to protest against the established system which is based on injustice and to expose the evil and hypocrisy of the higher castes. There is an urgent need to create a separate aesthetics for Dalit literature, an aesthetics based on the real experiences of life. "(The Aesthetics of Dalit Literature) In India it is under the pretext of the Caste and in the Western World it is under the name of the Race. Inequality is the main source of marginality which leads to insecurity, injustice and exploitation. In *Taming of Women* (2012) P. Sivakami vividly evokes a world where women and men are in constant conflict, scrambling for the little power to which they can hold on to. The protagonist Periyannan who is tyrannical and charismatic always tries to bring the women under his control. Derrida in his Deconstruction states about the Binary opposition "The problem with centers, for Derrida, is that they attempt to exclude. In doing so they ignore, repress or marginalize others (which become the other). In male-dominated societies, man is central (and woman is the marginalised other, repressed, ignored, pushed into the margins)."(22) Derrida in his Deconstruction says that "All of Western thought behaves in the same way, forming pairs of binary opposites in which one member of the pair is privileged, freezing the play of the system, and marginalizing the other member of the pair. (25) This paper will portray the sufferings and oppression faced by the marginalised women within the community under the pangs of men. In the society that is known as mainstream, the problems of Dalit women are considered separatist. They face the worst expressions of male chauvinistic society - atrocities like raping, profiling, physical assault and murder.

P. Sivagami born in 1957 is an acclaimed Tamil writer. The first Dalit woman to become a novelist she has written four critically acclaimed novels all of them centered on Dalit and feminist themes. In literary circles P.Sivakami is considered as a strong Dalit writer with a feminist penchant. She was secretary ranked bureaucrat in tamilnadu till 2008, the Indian posting gave her the opportunity to meet women and Dalit which led to social issues becoming sivaksamis concern and avocation. She is founder editor of literary magazine puthiya Kodangi. In 2009 she founded her own political party, samuga samathuva padai. In a literary world that was used to comfort and pleasure, Sivakami s novel slapped the reverie out of reading and forced the reader to face what was also real about this India we are living in: the touchy subject of caste and gender discrimination. P. Sivakamis background as a Dalit woman IAS officer, with close to 3 decades of workexperience in the field makes her the ideal person to have written the novel *The Taming Of Women* (2012). She writes from first-hand experience of the society she portrays, a life that at once feels familiar and alien to urban middle class readers. Originally written in Tamil, it has been translated into English by Pritham K. Chakravarthy. The essence of a lower socio-economic class with its trials and tribulations, the struggle for power across genders and class even that among peers, their thought processes – these have all come across in the translation

II

The Taming of Women, for the most part, portrays the discrimination between men and women in a small village. This is the story of hard-working Anandhayi, married to a womanizer, Periyannan, and their marital travails. There is struggle for power not only amidst genders, but generations and families within the village as well. Even peripheral characters like Anandhayis mother-in-law, Chinnasami, and Lakshmi are infused with originality. One of the most striking aspects of *The Taming of Women* is its humors. Sivakamis strength is in making the mundane not only amusing, but also painfully real. Periyannan is not content with the wealth that his farms bring him. He is hungry for the power that money can bring, and tyrannical in his treatment of the women in his life – be it his wife, his old and ailing mother, his daughters or the many women for whom he has an insatiable appetite. The opening chapter introduces this with a bang his wife Anandhayi gives birth while he has another woman with him upstairs, brought to him by the midwife with whom too, Periyannan often gets physical. Anandhayi has no illusions about him. She wishes, however, that he would not get his women home. As her daughters are growing up – who are inevitably affected by all that is going on around them. Later when he goes to town regarding work he falls in the beauty of Lakshmi and he is totally lost in her. And during his daughter marriage he brings her into the house and after some days he plays the same prangs which he does with Anandhayi and this makes a drift into their relationship. At first Anandhayi feels jealous for the women but after some days she becomes a great support to her. Due to the continuous misunderstandings between Periyannan and Lakshmi she plans to leave the house, thrice she leaves the house without his knowledge but he loses all his time power and money to bring her back home. Later they end in bad fight and lakshmi commits suicide. This hurts Periyannan a lot. As the day pass by his daughters reach the age of marriage and they do not have the freedom to select their life partner. As in the ancient times it was the women in Suyamvara had all the rights tochoose her own husband but when Periyannan finds his daughter in relationship with whom she preferred he abused her and gets her married to the men whom he preferred. The days went by and all his sons and daughters got married and settled. But still the attitude of Periyannan never changed. And the novel ends with Anandhayi being with her grandchildren and she thinks of the past life she knew every women he slept with. As long has he never hurt her she never worried of whom he was sleeping with.

III

In this novel the author portrays the real sufferings of the women among the men within the marginalised community. How the man struggle for power and sex and how the women are treated low and made to suffer physical ailments. The women characters in this novel either it be mother or wife or daughter or worker all are under the pangs of men, put under sufferings. Anandhayi the wife of Periyannan is about to give birth to a baby even at that time Periyannan is sleeping with another women in upstairs, a distant cousin had whispered secretly to her that "I saw machan last week near the blacksmith, with a woman"(1) she finds it and waits for her to get down. Anandhayi prays to god, saying "Sami....let the slut come down and she will get it from me. She who has climbed up has to climb down."(pg4) when she climbs down the stairs Anandhayi caught hold of her hair and shouts at her. Hearing it her mother-in-law the old crone wakes up and he comes rushing down the stairs to let the women lose from his wifes clutches and he pushes her. In the book *Why I am not a Hindu* kancha Ilaiah states that "When the father and mother quarrel, every aspect of life becomes public. No quarrel hides inside the house. For the children the house is a place of pleasure and of pain but it is all in the open." (20) Anandhayi falls to the ground with pain and she delivers the baby. But Periyannan never bothers about the cry of his wife he just leaves her and goes upstairs. He wakes up in the morning and goes out for work and only in the evening he comes home and sees the new born child...Anandhayi faces the struggle of bringing up her daughters Kala, Dhanam and Arul can be seen in these lines, "having a girl in the house is like having a fire in the belly... I will have peace only when I hand her over to a husband." (pg108) What all men need from the women is just physical pleasure either they select the women from their community or from other community and men see women only to fit into the household chores and produce baby.

Tomar mentions that R.S. Khare clearly argues that Dalit woman gear not only the personal and social dishonour but as well as the physical safety.

Within the home, Dalit woman often suffered from verbal and physical abuse at the hands of their fathers and brothers, raped by their father-in-law, or brother-in-law, forcefully subjugated to fulfil the pleasures of their husbands, domestic and sexual violence. They simultaneously dishonoured outside in public realm forced, unpaid in the economic sphere and often compounded by sexual harassment and a real risk to physical life.

When Periyannan is maintaining a secret relationship with Lakshmi he nags his wife by putting forth many question regarding her behaviors and beating her and abusing her. In *Untouchable God* the male character Namboodri as a brother-in-law thinks very low about his widowed Sister-in-law stating that

> "She must surely have been looking at men coming and going on the road. Hah! If I die, she will fly into the world of sex and romance like a bird with ten wings. Dont I know how these women are inside, never mind their fasts and mumbling? And then my brother will cast down from heaven. No chaste wife ought to be alive after the death of her husband: it only means shes secretly waiting for life to give her a chance at debauchery. Why else live? Better to enter the fire and purify the soul." (25)

No matter what ever the caste the women belong to but the thought of the men are the same. In order to hide their weakness for women they try to provoke that the women are having perverted mind and abuse them physically and mentally. Once when Periyannan returns home from work he finds a male near his house and without asking anything to him he beats him up thinking that he had secret relationship with Anandhayi and he asks about it to her for which she says "Your mind was always in gutter. The poor man is deaf. You beat him rashly and dare to call him my secret lover?"(59). Still he is not satisfied with her reply and he questions her to be arrogant for which she states that "Sure I sit home entertaining every passer-by. Who is here to stop me? Because you want to hide your shady doings, you are shifting the blame on me. How fair is that?" (59). Periyannan is least bothered about her and he says" Adiye, why the hell should I be scared of you? I only have to whistle and I can have any women I want. Do you know that?" (59).

Periyannan even ill treats his mother the old crone. In every way he never maintains a good contact with the women around him. Even to his daughters when they put forth their interests in studying he shows the anger to his wife. Periyannans daughters were denied education and they were only meant to do their household duties, get married and produce children and when he found his daughter reading a book which she got from her neighbor to study Periyannan forcefully took away the book and started ill-treating his wife and physically attacking her. Meena Kandasamy in *Their daughter*, she writes:

> Young wife near my father's home, with a drunken husband
> Who never changed; she bore his daily beatings until on one
> Stormy night, in fury, she killed him by stomping his seed bags...
> We: their daughters.
> We: the daughters of their soil.
> We, mostly, write. (14-19)

The women face sufferings even in the place where they work and even in the institution where they get education. Kanganis wifes sister Neelaveni who was known for her beauty in the village had many hidden rumors within her when she was sent to school she was physically trapped by the teachers and she faced many problems. Though it was her young age she was not aware of it finally she was made to quit her education, stay inside her home and was not allowed outside. In *Untouchable God* Kancha Ilaiah through the voice of the lower caste menstates that "There was a man called Manu many centuries ago, who wrote a book saying that lower-caste women should always offer themselves to the gaze of the upper-caste men. If they cover themselves, they will be assaulted and punished." (183) In each and every phase women are made to suffer a lot and men take hold of the situation and control them physically and mentally. Though periyannan illtreats the women in his life he feels that his fifth daughter fetches good luck for him so he never abuses her as he gets to know in the astrology that she will bring fortune and wealth to him he treats her with care. He abuses his mother, Anandhayi and Lakshmi but he never used harsh words for other women.

IV

Sivakami who is the first Tamil Dalit woman to write a novel does not mince words, her women suffer and they do not hide it; throughout the novel, Periyannan raises his hand on his wife and mistress and on occasion, even his daughter without a second thought. The women fight back viciously, and even exploit him for their own sexual pleasures and deny him when they so desire it; but in portraying the women's struggles as inevitable and, consequently, powerful in the way they startle the men who take them for granted. In fact, fidelity is not seen as an important quality by men, although the same behavior in females is cause for comment. The silent horrors of sexual harassment that occurs in daily life and its slithering invasion into the destruction of childhood innocence have been dealt with commendably.

Reference

1. Bharti, C.B., "The Aesthetics of Dalit literature," Trans. Darshana Trivedi. Hyati, June 1999.
2. Sivakami. P TheTaming of Women, New Delhi ,Thomson Press India Ltd. 2012. print
3. http://www.goodreads.com/book/show/15925032-the-taming-of-women
4. http://helterskelter.in/2012/09/book-review-the-taming-of-women/
5. http://www.sunday-guardian.com/bookbeat/an-eccentric-and-intriguing-ensemble-of-women
6. Ilaiah, Kancha. Untouchable God. Kolkata: Samya. 2013. Print.
7. Tomar, Ruchi. "Dalit Feminism: A Transformation of Rejection into Resistance." The Criterion 12 (2013): 1-8.

Chapter - IX

Untouchable God by Kancha Ilaiah:
A Thematic Study

Dalit literature represents the manifestations of the Dalit response to their exclusion from the main stream society, the caste based discrimination and untouchables. Dalit novel has its accomplishment in establishing alternative literature to Hindu dominated literature. Kancha Ilaiahs *Untouchable God* is the Dalit novel from Andra pradesh and it Potrays thereal life struggles of a community. The Proposition of the paper is to do a thematic study of Kancha Ilaiahs *Untouchable God* in the light of Caste, poverty, dominance, oppression and rivalry.

Key words: Caste, poverty, dominance, oppression and rivalry.

Paraiah, a Dalit is apparently beaten to death while walking about his village in the evening, allegedly for the crime of thinking about God, which might well lead to thoughts of equality. Six important men celebrate his death, which they had arranged. They represent the remarkable Brahmin of India. Veda Shastry of Tamilnadu is the rightful leader. Namboodri of Kerala is from a caste that created the most perfect system of discrimination that the world has seen; Krishnamurthy of Karnataka and Appa Rao of AndraPradesh are slightly moderate; Tilak of Maharastra dreams of increasing discrimination while Banerjee of Bengal believes he is above caste. Men take their leave from Shastry, lastly comes Isaiah, an American black, who knows all about race and journeys to India to find out about the non-violence movement that has inspired Martin Luther King, Jr., and discovers much more in India and leaves India with more memories.

Caste Discrimination

In this novel the caste discrimination can be seen evident between the upper caste Brahmin and the other inferior caste. The Paraiah were theworking class they have to work day and night without rest. They are squeezed till the last blood in their body. Paraiah had worked all day collecting the grains cut by women and bundling it so they could carry it away. Only an exceptional man like Paraiah did both male and female tasks.

> "Yet in the life of Paraiah no pleasure seems to exist. All the really important things he did, like killing the chicken or bundling the corps, were for others, not for him or his children. The only pleasure he tasted was that of feeding the corps with water and manure, and feeding his masters cattle. These acts marked him as a sinner, while his master, who owned both corps and cattle, but fed neither, was pure. The only truly pure thing, it seemed to him, was eating. The landlord ate for the benefit of the village, and the priest ate for the benefit of Gods." (4)

Paraiah felt sad because instead he suffered the endless pain that came when a human being was forced to lead the life of a dog. The Hindu Gods had failed to impress the divine separateness of caste on these dogs. The Brahmins lived in the other side of the village, far from this street. They lived in their divine feudal lands called agraharas. "The Gods gave those lands so they could stay away from the productive humans, socially connecting dogs and beasts of burden called donkeys." (5-6) The Hindu Gods has not stooped to create Chandalas, Paraiahs or dogs therefore the Brahmins hated them most. The Brahmins hated these things more than shit. The Brahmins felt that "God created the Brahmins from his head, the Kshatriyas from his shoulders, the Vaishyas from his thighs and the Shudras from his feet. The Panchamas-the filth-were unborn." (18) The Panchamas, of whom Paraiah was one, were never created by God. When Namboodri was travelling in bus He was distracted by the man who sat beside him and some of his parts touched Namboodri. He felt that "Evil days: A Brahmin gets touched so casually by an unknown, perhaps an untouchable! These buses are profane places" (23) When the upper caste men need a woman they would get over it from the lower caste family but they were considered to be untouchables. Namboodri was twenty he went to Govinda Nairs house and he spoke to him and he proposed his wish for marrying his daughter Sita Mahalaxmi. With this happy news he went to tell to his wife but his wife was weeping and said "My hopes are crumbled. Do you really wish her to live in sambandham? With all the namelessness my life is better: she will have neither face, nor name. She will be the mother of Brahmin children but shall remain an unwed Nair. Can her children become Brahmins, let alone Namboodris? Can they become priests in any temple? You foolishman, how could you agree?" (28). She disagree to give to Brahmins but Govindan Nair roared "A Brahmin-Namboodri- is a God of Gods on Earth. Whatever they ask, they ask only to increase our virtue. Our Gods said that Whatever a Brahmin asks, you must give it-whether it be wealth, cattle or daughter." (29) Govindan Nair said that as a spiritual demand he will give his daughter only to Namboodris and no one can stop it.

While the Brahmin justified whatever they did was right either it be food, women, work or sex. "A Brahmin enters into the sexual act not for the appetitites of his physical body but for the pleasure of God, while the Shudras, the untouchables, the tribals- the undivine archaic people- enter into the act only to have their own selfish bodily pleasure." (30) So they were not considered to be divine. Hence the sons born to those castes do not have the power to send the fathers soul to heaven. This was the reason why they remained Shudras, Chandalas and tribals. Aryavartha was the only country where the Gods exalted the spiritual sex. He was reminded of the Rig veda which contained slokas after slokas about how Indra, the God of Gods have loved women- not his wife of course- the apsaras, divine prostitute created by Gods to satisfy their own pleasure. "Occasionally he regretted that he had to perform his researches with such low material."

(35) When Balaram saw a priest sitting in the temple and teaching four children. He approached the priest and asked for his daughters education and the priest asked him which caste he belonged to and when he said he was Shudra the priest said

> "I am a pundit and priest of this temple. Above all I am a Brahmin. Do you think we teach Shudras, Chandalas, dogs and donkeys? Who let you march into the temple like this and ask me whether I would teach you low-born daughter-a girl, a damned bitch puppy! Get out! Out of this temple! Take your defiling feet off my floor!" (69).

The nine days of Ganesh was brought into the street. The Shudras distributed the Pamphlet. Some Paraiah came running to see the deity. Shudras stopped them and said "Dont come in here, you Paraiah Ganesh is a Hindu God. Not an Untouchable God." (97). Tilak came with his followers and said Ganesh will visit the Shudra street too. The Paraiah men shouted "We too have bodies. Are they not created by Gods? When the sounds of our drums is touchable for God why not our bodies?" (97). After the festival Tilak invited all the people and told the tolerance behind the plan he told them briefly that one of the Brahmin is being arrested by the police and the Muslims are high in number we have to stimulate the lower caste Shudras and tell them that the Muslim men attacked their men in the market place and if the rivalry between them broke out our Brahmin would be released and the investigation will turn upon the Shudras. He asked the people to heat the Shudras with passion and righteousness. "No Brahmin boy should go to jail."(91) When Isaiah asked his doubt about their semi-naked status for which Jacob said "There was a man called Manu many centuries ago, who wrote a book saying that lower-caste women should always offer themselves to the gaze of the upper-caste men. If they cover themselves, they will be assaulted and punished."

(183) He further said that Manu also said that Dalit should not own property, gold or ornament. They have to cook only in broken pot and eat in mutilated bowls. Elumalai narrated hoe the upper caste men made use of the lower caste women while saying this his eyes became red "not from drinking liquor but from drinking history... the history of untouchable slavery ... the history of womens untouchable bodies and touchable private parts." (192). Elumalai, Jacob and Isaiah went to see the Shiva temple the upper caste people started attacking them with stones and Elumalai got hurt. When they saw Isaiah coming they said "An untouchable with a black devil was coming towards their Gods!" (198). Jacob and Isaiah went to book shop to purchase some book he took book on Rig Veda. He read some word in the book

> "God has made the caste: the Brahmins from his head, the Kshatriyas from his shoulders and arms, the Baniyas from his belly and the Shudras from his feet. The untouchables and women werent mentioned at all. He remembered the words of Genesis: So God created man as his own image. In the image of God created He him, Male and Female created He them" (212).

Inferior Vs Superior

Men always considered them to be the superior and they considered the women to be of low birth and they were considered to be inferior. Several women were returning home after the long days labour work. Harvesting the crops was mostly a female task.

> "Men were men whatever caste they were born in; they tilled the land and fed the cattle but they would never cook, or weed crops. The division between the labour of men and women was so deep that it was almost a thing of nature; it was so old that no one could have said whether it was made by Gods or humans." (1)

In the priest Veda Shastrys house in the kitchen the women were wearing wet sari around their shivering bodies and cooking it gives satisfaction to Gods and they were preparing thirty three different dishes. The youngwomen cutting the vegetable in the kitchen felt that "All the hours of the day we sulk in this rat hole of a kitchen, cooking nasty food that we will never eat. We can only know how our food tastes from our mens praise or blame. I think Shudra women, Chandala women are better off than us." (12) Veda Shastry felt we must look for alternative arrangement for producing children. He said that there was once a king called Nala who was born in male's womb as his father coupled with another male. He said

> "If we could cultivate the habit of men mating with men, we could remove pollution from our lives forever. As it is we are constantly in peril from the filthy stink of women. They are liable to bleed at any time and destroy the sanctity of the sacrifice and the integrity of mediation; their wombs are poison cells." (15-16)

Appa Rao had a doubt that why do women cook in wet clothes? Our Gods enjoyed the food cooked by men in times past. For which Veda Shastry smiled and said the same Nala who was born of a man was the finest cook in Aryavartha. He always cooked in wet clothes even Bhima was an excellent cook thats why Nala and Bhima are always praised first. The food was being served and people ate the food Veda Shastry said "As we are inadequately manly we are forced to eat food prepared by spiritually polluted beings- women" (18). The women in Veda Shastrys house were well trained. They were unobtrusive as ghosts, yet always alert for unexpected emergencies. They knew that if they committed mistake in the home, they would be punished by the law of Dharma- just as Panchamas were punished for mistakes in the public sphere. Even in the upper caste houses only the leftover food were eaten by the women. When Isaiah came to Dalit colony when they were having food only the men ate first when the women was asked to sit and dine " No, no We women do not eat till all the men in the house have eaten" said Veeramma (194). When Isaiah says that in our case men and women sit together and eat but and he said that "Our women eats more than we men eat". (195) Veeramma gives reply to Isaiah that "NO woman eats more than men. Men eat all the food and say we did not eat". (195)

Sexual workers/ Widow

The women of the upper caste and lower caste are treated as sexual dolls and concubines by men. They simply use them and throw away. Thought the women who belong to lower caste are called untouchable but their body is touchable and they can be used as the men wish. Namboodri a Brahmin was twenty he went to Govinda Nairs house and he spoke to him and he proposed his wish for mating his daughter Sita Mahalaxmi. With this happy news he went to tell to his wife but his wife was weeping and said "My hopes are crumbled. Do you really wish her to live in sambandham? With all the namelessness my life is better: she will have neither face, nor name. She will be the mother of Brahmin children but shall remain an unwed Nair. Can her children become Brahmins, let alone Namboodris? Can they become priests in any temple? You foolish man, how could you agree?" (28). She disagree to give to Brahmins but Govindan Nair roared "A Brahmin-Namboodri- is a God of Gods on Earth. Whatever they ask, they ask only to increase our virtue. Our Gods said that Whatever a Brahmin asks, you must give it-whether it be wealth, cattle or daughter."

(29) Govindan Nair said that as a spiritual demand he will give his daughter only to Namboodris and no one can stop it. Sita overheard the conversation and started weeping. By spending time around her mother she has learnt a lot about the world of women. But that world had no status of its own.

The day came where he and Sita were alone in the room and it was their first night. He experimented all the sixty four arts and it continued for many days and he said this is what Rama did to Sita and Vishnu did to Laxmi. She was forced to sleep with that monkey Namboodri. She begot three kids for him. Aryavartha was the only country where theGods exalted the spiritual sex. He was reminded of the Rig veda which contained slokas after slokas about how Indra, the God of Gods have loved women- not his wife of course- the apsaras, divine prostitute created by Gods to satisfy their own pleasure. He asked her how do you like this life Sita? She replied "I live the life of a dog, shut in a kennel, whelping every so often. When my master caresses me, I fawn on him," (39). Namboodris sister-in-law Shiva Shakthi who was sitting on the verandah saw him coming she ran into the home like a rat that see the snake glides into the rat hole. She was a permanent widow her head was shaven and she weared mundu and her breast was covered with white pallu. Her days went in doing laboring in kitchen with wet clothes. Her relatives and other widows told her that she must not feel happy and free when she is alone but she really felt free in the absence of her dreadful brother-in-law. Namboodris elder brother died two years ago he believed in sati, though it was not under practice he couldnt do anything. He felt that

> "She must surely have been looking at men coming and going on the road. Hah! If I die, she will fly into the world

of sex and romance like a bird with ten wings. Dont I know how these women are inside, never mind their fasts and mumbling? And then my brother will cast down from heaven. No chaste wife ought to be alive after the death of her husband: it only means shes secretly waiting for life to give her a chance at debauchery. Why else live? Better to enter the fire and purify the soul." (25)

When Isaiah comes to Benares he asks Jacob who are these women with white sari and their heads clean shaved Jacob says "They are widows, they come here to live. They have nowhere else to go. Their families sent them here." (232) Only the upper caste widows were burnt on pyres, because upper caste men feared they might pollute the familys bloodline." Women cannot become Brahmins? The scriptures regard them as Shudras, unclean. Bankim Chandra called widowhood a Vishbriksha a tree of poison." (238) Then he meets Mala she does research over there and she explains to him about the women she says that all the girls are widow. Some of them look no older than ten. In spite of the law the people will marry off their girls very young some time too much older men, they become widows inevitably and then they are packed off on pilgrimage to Varanasi or kasha from which they are not indented to return. The lower caste women were treated as concubine they were made to clean the temple and they were forced to sleep with the temple priest. "No doubt that the men who control the ashrams feel like kings with enormous harems to boss around. They count theirwealth in womens bodies. This is not as extreme or perverted as you might think: women have been an item of exchange for centuries." (240).

Education for women

Balaram and his wife Sakku Bai, had a dream. It was the dream of educating their only daughter Saraswathi as they named her after the Hindu Goddess of Learning. Balaram was a fruit vendor and his wife was doing daily wages. On the way Balaram saw a priest sitting in the temple and teaching four children. He approached the priest and asked for his daughters education and the priest asked him which caste he belonged to and when he said he was Shudra the priest said

> "I am a pundit and priest of this temple. Above all I am a Brahmin. Do you think we teach Shudras, Chandalas, dogs and donkeys? Who let you march into the temple like this and ask me whether I would teach you low-born daughter-a girl, a damned bitch puppy! Get out! Out of this temple! Take your defiling feet off my floor!" (69).

Pir sahib asked Sakku the reason for the long face while cleaning the mosque and she explained what had happened. He asked her to send her daughter to Jahanara bee she has studied till eight standard and she can teach the basic letters. Saraswathi carried her books and along with it a broom sticks so that people would think she is going for cleaning work. Mala tells to Isaiah how her Parents accepted to do her Ph.D only when she told her parents that she would marry whomever they show as bridegroom but she should be allowed to do her Ph.D. she even explains the state of other women how even the present generation girls didnt even learn their letters. "Till recently it was believed that if a girl tempted the fates, such as by learning to read, she would cause her husbands death." (238)

Poverty

Paraiah had worked all day collecting the grains cut by women and bundling it so they could carry it away. "Only an exceptional man like Paraiah did both male and female tasks." The Paraiah men was described as

> "He was black as buffalo, his hair was longish and he had no upper garment, only a loincloth round his waist. Of medium height, he had a slight, rather sparse beard. The boniness of his frame was unmitigated by muscle, and

his skin, robbed early of its natural tautness, hung in wrinkles." (2)

Weariness bent his limbs like Lord Rama s bow, but his soul appeared heavier. He felt more pain when the landlord asked him to kill chicken, but he longed to taste the chicken curry but to the end he would only get only the bones as reward for thr slaughter. The landlords family would get flesh because they never committed the sin of cutting the birds throat. "They, the givers of orders and the eaters, were sacred: he, the slayer and the ordered, was not. Sacredness appeared and disappeared like sunshine." (4) He felt that pleasure and pain turn the wheel of life.

"Yet in the life of Paraiah no pleasure seem to exist. All the really important things he did, like killing the chicken or bundling the corps, were for others, not for him or his children. The only pleasure he tasted was that of feeding the corps with water and manure, and feeding his masters cattle. These acts marked him as a sinner, while his master, who owned both corps and cattle, but fed neither, was pure. The only truly pure thing, it seemed to him, was eating. The landlord ate for the benefit of the village, and the priest ate for the benefit of Gods." (4)

The summer days of Paraiah went on starving and they would feed on the dead cattle which died of airborne disease. The hope of chicken or mutton would go unmet for years and in some families it would go thus for a generation. Paraiah felt sad because "Instead he suffered the endless pain that came when a human being was forced to lead the life of a dog." (4) Paraiah dreamt that his children and the dogs were fighting over the same bones. He did not ever want to see that day in real life. Basu surveyed a meeting he said we are gathered here to learn of comrade Sanyals experience in the western tribal belt of Bengal and his success in widening the ambit of the party. Sanyal spoke that he has not come to share his experience as he himself is a part of laboring and suffering humanity. He said he came to speak of Hunger. To feel hungers true bite one must be born hungry.

> "Why, it is a great and shameful paradox of our society that it is the very people who produce food, clothing, shelter, utensils, who clean ourselves and our surroundings, even those who cart water, the most essential commodity of life. They are the ones with the least entitlement of life." (123)

Isaiah saw people semi dressed and they were begging and he asked about it to Jacob "They are begging for money replied Jacob. "Almost all of them come from Dalit and other lower-caste families. They dont have anything to live on. Hence they beg." (183) Manu the ancient Hindu law maker said that Dalit should not own property, gold or ornament. Theyhave to cook only in broken pot and eat in mutilated bowls and now because of Dravida Khazagam movement gradual change is taking place. The Dalit houses, by and large, had crumbling mud walls, thatched roofs and were fronted with a platform plastered with red mud or cattle dung. The men and women surrounded him and they told that God who looked like Shiva had come to their colony. "God never come to our colony said one women with graying hair" (187). Nakedness and semi-nakedness were part of the lives of the people in the colony. The Dalit people felt that they were able to clean the houses of upper caste people but due to poverty they were not able to take care of themselves.

Reference

1. Ilaiah, Kancha, Untouchable God. *Kolkata: Samya,* 2013.Print
2. Nimbalkar Waman. Dalit literature:Nature and Role. Nagpur: Prabodhan Prakashan. 2006. Print.

Chapter - X

Joseph Macwan's Step Child: A Thematic study

Dalit literature is an attempt to examine the aspects of Marginalisation, oppression, discrimination and the Dalit response in the forms of resistance and rebellion. The history of resistance and rebellion of Dalit did not form the part of historiography, art and literature. Dalit literature represents the manifestations of the Dalit response to their exclusion from the main stream society, the caste based discrimination and untouchables. Dalit novel has its accomplishment in establishing alternative literature to Hindu dominated literature. Joseph Macwans *Step Child* is the first Dalit novel from Gujarat and it Potrays the real life struggles of a community. The Proposition of the paper is to do a thematic study of Joseph Macwans Step Child in the light of Caste, poverty, dominance, oppression and rivalry.

Key words: Caste, poverty, dominance, oppression and rivalry.

Angaliyat focuses mainly on the Vankar community but the narrativedevelopes around the structure of domination where the Patidar calls all the shots. The novel opens with two hardworking and simple Vankar friends who, motivated by a deep sense of dignity, confront Patidar youth when they make advances to a Vankar girl in the neighbouring village. The incident is followed by a series of conflicts with the dominant community and ultimately both friends sacrifice their lives. A black sheep named Ramlo from within the

Vankars who support the oppressive Patidar offsets the class between good and evil. Macwans narrative skills are both engaging and complex, sharply pointing out the enemy within and without.

Caste discrimination

The novel is about the community of weavers, the Vankars, is subject to oppression from the more powerful upper caste of the Patels. When Teeho and Valji went for auction in Shilapaar they come across the incident where an upper caste man threw a stone on the pot of charming young women she was drenched and abashed and around her feet the broken pot was shattered. This humiliated Teeho and he went forward to question the men who casted the stone and he belonged to the Patels. But the men and his companions said to him that "you mind your own business, outsider! The fellow raised his voice to snub Teeho" (16). But Teeho attacked the upper caste men and his companions. The trouble makers companion got angry and came forward to attack Teeho "A low-caste man publicly humiliating an upper-caste , a patel no less! How could anyone allow this? "(16). Teeho grabbed him by the collar and threw him around. Valji took the measuring rod in his hand and waited to deal with other three fellows. The village mukhi arrived to the spot and he was aware of the situation and its happenings. Megho Patel told the mukhi that "You are the mukhi. I want to file a police complaint against this *dhed* (low-caste). The situation went out of control and the upper caste men started attacking Teeho and he was wounded with blood stain. Teeho felt so bad that no one came forward to say "Teehabhai, you have saved us from disrepute" he understood that no one wanted to be on the wrong side of the patidars.

> "Teeho was aware of this in fact it filled him with contempt. The entire mohalla consisted of eighty houses. If all of them stood united, the twenty-five families of the patels would be powerless, but if they couldnt even dream of

standing up for themselves, how were they to face the patels? The money was with the patels, Infact, as far as money was conserned, even the Thakore depended upon the Patels. In such circumstances to pick a fight with them was impractical and foolish" (18).

On the way Methi met him and invited him to his house it was for the girl whom he picked up the fight. In her home Moti her bother said that "But you know how it is- first of all our caste is a low one, and then one cant live in water and risk enmity with the crocodile" (19). While in the village square the upper caste men were in a rage "The Patels argued that if a low-caste man and an outsider at that, had publicly beaten up a Patels son, he must be taught a lesson for life" (26). In India it is under the pretext of the Caste and in the Western World it is under the name of the Race. Inequality is the main source of marginality which leads to insecurity, injustice and exploitation.

Rival between the upper caste and lower caste:

The enmity which started in Shilapaar when Teeho attacked the Patels it arose to many problems in and around the villages the Patels destroyed the land of Heera Khana and they hung a threatening note that

> "If you have anything to do with any of your community members in Ratnappar or let any of them enter here, that will be your end. You will be thrown out of the village, without even a drop of water from the lake. If you wish to live in this village harmoniously, then let Moti Dhula and Heera Khana be ostracized and made to answer for their conduct!" (29).

The Patels were agitated with the issue of Teeho attacking them and they wanted to take revenge on him so they were desperate to ruin Teehas life. The love which Methi and Teeho had developed were know to these people and they were waiting for good time to spoil it "She goes around like a sati, let her be saddled with this one, it will straighten her up for life. If Teeha has to live this knowledge, his life will be miserable. There is no punishment wore than this" (38). The evil intention of raping Methi underwent a change instead they planned to ruin her future. They called Methis child marriage husband Chunthia and they told him that "we have heard that Heera is not arranging the aanu and somebody from another paragna is making plans to elope with your wife. The caste may be yours, but our village will earn a bad reputation! This kind of thing had never happened before in any caste. We have not let it happen. And even now we dont want it to happen" (39). For which Chunthia never agreed and said "You think I am a worm, dont you? Who asked you to take the responsibility of my aanu? I spit on your money...! His words infuriated Meghi, his nephew manji and his worthless son Nanio and Nanji said "Look at that! What arrogance for a bloody dhedh!" (40).

A sly farmer from Keradia gave those people a helping hand and he got a mean-looking wizened man with filthy thoughts murmuring some idea to them and they carried out the plan well to ruin Methi and Teehas wedding. When Valji planned to make a secret way to fix Methis wedding he asked Dano to help for fixing the taxi to bring Methi in the night but when they approached Gola he never accepted for helping them even when they accepted to pay thrice the amount. Then Dano remembered the help which Dhelavala promised he will do when he caught him in the night with Ramlo he never spread about it to the villagers so Dhelavala said "Look Dana, you seem to be a useful person. Ask for my help when you are struck someday. I will not turn you down" (72). So he approached him but he tooplayed a cunning role by giving a helping hand but he spread the message to Meghiji and the plan got collapsed and instead of Dano and Valji it was Manji and Nanji taking Methi to Keradia and when Valji tried to rescue her he was beaten to death. When Dano approached Heera to talk about Teehos acceptance for their daughters wedding the secret plan made by the upper caste people was revealed which ruined both Methi and Teehas future. Heera showed the letter written by Teeha to Methi stating her to get married and not to wait for him anymore but it was the plan of the patels and it was they who wrote secret letter to Methi. After this letter Methi got married to Chunthia and Teeho remained unmarried. Even after so many years once when Teeha went into the town for auction when Dano and Jeeva was not there he was beaten up to death. "Eight to ten young men came crushing down upon Teeha. With sticks and punches, they left Teeha half dead." (226).

Friendship

The friendship between Teeho, Valji, and Bhavankaka was immortal. Though they had small misunderstanding still they stick together as good friends. It was so that even they fight badly the people in the village stated that "If one were to see them in that state, one would have thought that they never saw eye to eye. But these two were an unusual pair. Inseperable, two bodies with single soul". (2) Valji settled down to married life and he wants Teeho also to get married and when his wife Kanku insisted on giving her sister to Teeho, Valji felt happy but he was too much bothered weather Teeho will accept for that proposal or not. One day he put forth the proposal to Teeho but he never accepted and it and it lead to fight between them and Valji promised that he would not step into his threshold nor see his face again but the next day morning as soon as the rooster crew valji went towards Teehos house such was the friendship between them.

Bhavankaka helped them and gave moral support to them always he was the man behind them in taking decisions for their life. It was Bhavankaka who went to Heeras house to speak about Teehos wedding with Methi and it was he who stood behind Teeho after the loss of his parents. "Bhavankaka was only one who stood by Teehas convictions" and it was "only two person in the entire village could engage Teeha in plain speaking. One was valo and other Bahvankaka" (3).

When Teeho refused for marriage no one knew the reason behind it and Kanku started teasing valji "so much for friendship, didnt even know what was going on his friends life" (4). Even after the fight which they had in Shilapaar they went in different direction to safe guard their life and when they met each other to be safe they hugged eachother. And when Valji found out that Teeho is in love with Methi he said he will arrange for the wedding and he put his heart and soul to bring the wedding done. Unfortunately he passed away due to the secret plans made by the patels. It was a great loss to Teeho. He states to Kanku that "Youve become a widow in a worldly sense I have become a widower in another" (118). Even after so many years the rage in the hearts of the upper caste men was not reduced. When Teeho entered the village with his son for auction he was brutally beaten to death. After this Bhavankaka left the village and no one knew about him after that.

Love and Marriage

The love and marriage portrayed in this novel is so intense and the relationships are very loyal to each other. The love between Teeho and Methi is so intense and they fall in love with each other at first sight though they belong to different paragna they go to the extent of marrying each other. At first Teeho fights and rescues Methi when an upper caste man threw a stone at the pot she carried and from then on the vengeance between the caste starts and it leads to loss of many people. Though Teeho is not allowed to enter Shilapaar but instead of him his close friends Valji and Bahavankaka make a visit to Heeras house to fix the wedding it was at that time when Heera was in dialemma to give assurance for the wedding as there was enmity within the villages it was Methi who say to Bhavaankaka "There is very little traffic between our villages. I may not be able to send a message again; on the noon of the next full moon day, I shall be waiting for him, like Okha, here by the fallow land. Hire a van, if need be, and rescue me!" (57).

Valji got the taxi to get Methi but Manji and Nanji took over the situation and they got Methi in the taxi and went straight to Keradia. When Valji went to rescue her he was crushed to death. When Kanku asks Teeho to give acceptance to Methi s marriage he says

> "Teeho has taken an oath bhabhi, if you have denied yourself the world in your widowhood, I have denied myself my desires in the separation from my friend. Youve become a widow in a worldly sense, I have become a widower in another. Not Methi alone, but that very direction has become inimical to my existence. Bring that up again over my dead body" (118).

Even after so many years Methi waited for Teehos acceptance for marriage but an upper caste men wrote a false letter to Methi as it was from Teeho, stating her not to wait and to go on to her in-laws house to Keradia.

Even after so many years after the desperate life with Chunthia when Methi is about to commit suscide it was Teeho who rescues her and her child and gives shelter and safeguards them. Even at that point of time they never felt like starting life together. As far as concerned the love between Teeho and Methi was not just physical it was more of pure eternal love. Kanku proved to be a best better half for valji she supported him a lot. Valji understood his wife that "she wasnt just his wife, but his true companion. Very practical, extremely affectionate and truly committed to his happiness.On the whole, she was more concerned about others, rather than herself" (4). She mourned a lot for his death. It was Teeho who gave consoling words for Kanku "you need grit to give up mourning, Bhabhi. The mother who weans the child away from her breast suffers more than the child itself; but for the childs own good she has to toughen herself. How long will you grive?" (106).

And there came a time that Dano should take care of Kanku and her son as it was the last promise of Valji to Dano but earlier Kankus sister's marriage was fixed with Teeho since Teeho refused to do so the next preference was Dano. While Dano proved to be a good companion, trustable cousin of Valji. It was after his death Dano took care of Kanku and Valjis son. Dano refused to Marry Kankus sister because the society will misinterpret the life of Kanku, Dano and Monghi. When Jeevan asks about it, Dano asks himself to put into his situation and see and he asks him to marry Monghi "if my marrying solves your problem, then why just Monghi, for your sake, I would marry even a witch" (126). Then they fix the marriage between Jeevan and Monghi and after their marriage Teeho tells Dano to marry Kanku as it was a great shock to him at first he refuses and he starts to attack Teeho and when he sees Kanku he stops and asks Teeho to repeat whatever he has told him. Teeho was frozen but later he spoke "He was bent upon bringing Methi over. I reminded him of my oath and said that if you want me to marry; you should first marry Kankubhabhi only then will I marry" (130). And later Kanku gave assurance of what Teeho said was true "You have not realised what he must have gone through before saying this much to you, Dana, and so you have sinned by hurting him. If you wish to safeguard your brother's dignity, marry me. Neither you, me, nor Teehabhai has any alternative left" (131). Even though they had many chances to get into physical they maintained decorum and they proved to be with high qualities and later on when Dano felt what Kanku told was right he accepted for the wedding and they got married.

Methi started her life with Chunthia after receiving the false letter of Teeho from the uppercaste. But the marriage didnt work out well she hadundergone many problems to make her life secure but right after the delivery of her first child her husband started treating her very badly and it went to extent that when Methi tried to safe guard her child from her husband she hit on him so badly and came to a state to finish off her life. It was at that time that Teeho rescued her and gave her shelter and later on due to her pestering Teeho accepted for marriage and he married Vali a cousin of Kanku.

The act of Bravery

Teeho proved his courage to the upper caste people not only once but twice. He questioned the atrocity which the upper caste did and when he went for auction to Shilapaar. A bull ran into the bazaar. Seein it snorting and rushing towards them, people ran helter-skelter. But Teeho caught hold of its hump and he tightened its reins and dug his heels into bulls side within half an hour the bull was panting and had frothing in the mouth "Finally it just collapsed. Teeho sprang from its back. There was no fight left in the bull, it meekly allowed Teeho to remove the bale form its back" (12). And from that day Teehos reputation in the district grew and it was due to his bravery he was not harassed by the robbers. The second incident was when a stone was casted on the pot which a girl carried and when she was drenched in water Teeho questioned the man who did such unjust thing. Even after knowing that it was uppercaste men he was dare enough to pick up fight with them and he attacked the troublemaker and his companions and he was brought to the village square at that time he withdrew the sword and told mukhi "Thakore, it is your responsibility to ensure that this bundle reaches me. Any true son of his mother may come forward. This bhavani sword knows no friends today" (27). He held his sword high and he ran through the fields and he tied his sword to his waist and climbed the hillock there he found eight young scoundrals he whirled the stump round and round in the air and aimed at them and it hit almost all people. The scoundrel Nanio ran for his life "Teeho chased him and jumped on him. Upon seeing Deaths own messanger before him, sheer fright loosened the fellow's sphincter"(28). When Manji and Nanji took over Mehti it was Valji who ran into the fields to rescue Methi he chased the car and he tried his best to attack Gola and bring the car to halt but he failed and he was crushed to death. Even till the last moment he never gave up he gave his life as a sacrifice to his friend. Even after many years when Teeho stepped into shilappar for auction he was attacked by eight to ten people, even at the last moment he fought with them to safeguard himself but he failed to do so and he passed away.

Support of the law

The uppercaste people though they can do anything with money and power but in this novel whoever does the crime are being punished while the law never works in favour of the caste, power, or people. When the uppercaste people destroyed the fields of Heeras fields with the help of Master Valji and Teeho met the Collector and explained the whole incidents which took palce in Shilapaar. The next day police came to arrest the people who destroyed the field and asked Teeho to give the names of the people without fear of who attacked him and destroyed the fields of Heera. For which Teeho replied

> "To tell the truth Saheb, I am not at all afraid of anybody. Why should I be afraid when we have a government of people like you. If they cronfront me one at a time I would relish even dying in the process. Its just that difficult to cope with the harassment of our people ans conspiracies that take place behind our backs" (48).

When Valji was killed the police went to Keradia and rescued Methi and arrested the people who were behind the death of Valji.

> "Manji, Nanji and Gola were found guilty on the charges of conspiracy and execution of the murder of Valji, and were sentenced for life. Dehlavala was made to serve internment for a month and a half and charged with a fine of 1000 rupees for playing an indirect role in the conspiracy. On the other hand, Meghji patel and Khushlo were given the benefit of doubt since there was no evidence of their direct and indirect involvement" (105).

When the riot between Jeevan and Dehlavalas car driver Ramlo broke out there was a huge rage in Ratnapaar. The people started attacking each other and they were searching for Jeevan with blood rage. Dano Jeevan and Teeho went to master and told about the whole situation. Master picked them to police station the DSP never responded properly to the situation since they were under Dehlavalas control. Master asked the driver to go to Ahmedabad the car reached Gandhijis ashram. Master went and met Gandhijis senior followers and told about the happenings in Ratnapaar and about Dehlavala. Within that day all arrangements were made and a letter from Regional President reached Dehlavala it stated that he should ask forgiveness to the vankarvas and later it will be reported whether he will be allowed to continue or dismiss the party. Before Master left he said to Dehlavala that" The sun of Gandhi Bapu is still warm in this country, Dehlavala "(201).

Conclusion

The Dalit novel has limited number of Characters. It reveals the unexplored issues of Indian society which are excluded by the main stream Indian English Writers. It talks about Dalit victimisation and identity movements. The protagonist of the Dalit novel is the community itself. It highlights the cultural silence imposed on the Dalits and tries to break the silences rightly empowering the Dalits. Further, it succulently explores the Gender bias being practiced in India. Joseph Macwan s *Step Child* is the first Dalit novel to be written and it portrays the Dalit suffering and narrates the hardship of a Dalit life.

Reference

1. Macwan, Joseph. Step Child. New Delhi: Oxford. 2004. Print.
2. Nimbalkar Waman. Dalit literature:Nature and Role. Nagpur: Prabodhan Prakashan. 2006. Print.

Chapter - XI

Thematic study of Sharankumar Limbale's Novel Hindu

This novel *Hindu* seeks to highlight the power politics and further consequences that lead to the killing of a Dalit youth, raping of a Dalit woman and further legal operations from both the caste Hindus and the Dalits is all the novel about. Under the rules of reservation of seats in politics, the post of the village sarpanch falls to their share. When the dalit activist gets the attention through the performance of jalasa the upper caste men are not able to tolerate it. They plan a secret murder and then they murder the Dalit activist. Later on the novel takes many forms and the Dalit activist brother takes the role in hand with the help of the upper caste men and he gets into politics and he reaches the position to rule the state. The preposition of the paper is to highlight the effectiveness of each Dalit characters and the themes of the novel in a assertive way.

Key words: Dalits, violence, murder, rape.

Social Back Ground of the Novel

Sharankumar Limabale the author of the book shares his thoughts of the evolution of the novel Hindu as he states that "The fabric of Hindu society, interwoven with inequality, and the disfigurement of the caste system- Hindu has been written to perform a post mortem of these two. Our country cannot become beautiful until the stain of the caste system is washed away from its face" (xii Hindu) The novel Hindu appeared first in Marati in the year 2003 and later on it was translated into Hindi, Malayalam and to English. Sharankumar Limbale further adds that Hindu is not just a literary text, but also about my literary role. It is my response to the casteist climate of our country. Hindus propelling event is the murder of a Dalit activist by a group of higher caste villagers because he had become too big for his boots in their eyes and through his Ambedkaraite theatre wasthreatening the established order by inciting his caste members, Mahars, to convert. Arun Prabha Mukeerje states that "Dalit writing as a whole, and Hindu, in particular, challenges the claim of universality made by the mainstream high caste writers and its critics by pointing out that they either ignore dalits together or misrepresent them" (xv-Hindu).

Setting

The story revolves around the setting of Alachpur. It is a place with beatiutiful surroundings, dotted by hills. It is the place which holds three thousand as its population and has a village Panchayat also. Alachpur is old village with recently developed primary school and post office. The two land mark of the village are the hangman hills in which the British hanged lot of Indians during their rule and the other is the Kavales baras elevation in which the whole village can be seen. Effective characters in the novel are Tatya Kamble, Sadanand Kamble, Madhukur Kavale, Prabhakar Kavale, Gopichand, Manikchand.

Themes

Caste and Political Conflict

The Caste discrimination in Hindu is depicted clearly through politics. In this novel Hindu Kasbe tells that there is a talk about Prabhakar Kamble becoming the next patil, the head man of the village. As Rambhau Kamble will retire in about two years then "Tatya Kamble will get a chance as the post will be reserved for dalit candidates as by law" (4). But Rambhau Kavale will never step down the village headship which his family has enjoyed. He will make sure that his son becomes the next patil.

Sonali the daughter in law of Rambhau Kavale went upstairs to see the jalsa being performed by Tatya Kambale. For first time she felt that speech was like erupting volcano. The people were waiting to murder Tatya Kamble at the village square. Prabhakar Kavale, Gunvant Patil, Jagannath Pandit, Balshetwar were hiding and they came running out with weapons in their hands, and pounced upon Tatya Kamble. But somehow he got out of their clutches but Shankar Pujari grabbed him as he started to scream the village doors began to close one after the other, Prabhakar had a sword, Gunvant had a spear, Jagannath Pandit an axe and others had knife. Sonalis heart sank as she saw the massacre. At that precise moment Manikchand and Gopichand car arrived on the scene and the violent crowd dispersed. Tatya Kamble fell on the ground. Sonali froze and she walked down the stairs slowly. The crowd broke out and they were scattered in different places.

Manikchand car came near the gate of Rambhau and told that he saw his son murdering Tatya Kamble. And they made a secret dealing not to reveal it to anyone.

Miland seated in the car with Gopichand and Manikchand was on the way to enjoy the night .The car crossed Bhimnagar decorated with buntings and banner. Suddenly the headlight of the car showed the agitated crowd and Murder shouted Manikchand. Tatya Kambles blood soaked body was twitching by the roadside get the car moving shouted Manikchand. And car speeded up to Rambhau Kavales house. Miland said to him that there has been a Murder. And asked where was his son Prabhakar? For which patil told that he has gone to Pune to visit his brother Madhukar. Then he said to Kavale that he saw him in the crowd. Kavales face turned pale.

Behind him stood his eldest son Sudhakar making odd gestures. He was mentally retarded. But hiding his emotions Kavale called them to dine with him tonight because they were his guest. For which Miland got shocked his eyes filled with tears and thought of Tatya Kamble. He was like a lion. The killers have erased the identity of the village as Jalsakar Tatya Kambles village forever. He felt that "This was an attempt to teach a lesson to ordinary dalits by killing a dalit. Who was respected for his talents and had made a name for himself. It was the disfigured face of social terrorism. Dalits have been murdered for thousands of years."(12).

Manikchand said that Tatya Kamble was murdered and who knows where his brother Sadananad Kamble might be so we came for nothing tonight he said. "Kavale has removed the thorn called Tatya Kamble. Now he can have his son anointed as patil" said Gopichand. (12). Then Miland felt that now the law is on the Dalit side and the person who murdered him will surely go to jail. But paying the money they will get bail said Manikchand. Then Miland asked himself many questions was he dead or alive? Is he an activist or not a man? How can he be quite for the murder of Tatya Kamble? The car entered the farmhouse. Sadananad Kamble came running to open the gate he works as a watchman. He was Tatya Kambles brother he was not aware of the murder. He felt like holding him and weeping on his shoulders. But Manikchand strictly said to him not to say it to Sadananad because when he comes to know about the murder he will run into the village and he too will be killed so Miland kept quite.

Miland told them to tell Sadananad about the murder for which they said "Miland, we dont know what we witnessed to this event. Remember the three monkeys of Gandhi."(16). Prabhakar Kavale came into the room with blood rage. And caught hold of Manikchand legs and asked him not toreveal that he saw him at the murder spot. And Manikchand told that he wont do it and Prabhakar Kavale drank the wine in the glass and ate the mutton and he said to them that for seventy generations of Tatya Kamble family lived off the scraps which they discharged. But he did not respect our charity. The words of Prabhakar Kavale struck Miland and said to him that he will reveal about him to the police and get him handcuffed. For which they both fought with each other. Miland felt that "Muslims dont kill dalits, nor do Christians. Buddhist doesnt commit atrocities on dalit, nor do Sikhs. Then why do Hindus torment dalits? Dont they accept the dalits are Hindu too? (27). Rohit Kamble the son of Tatya Kamble lit the pyre. Tatya Kamble body turned to ashes in a moment. There was a total silence.

The laws being in favor of the people. The police visited Kavales Bara and every one were nervous. Then constable Marathe asked Rambhau Kavale about Prabhakar but he told that he was in pune. And the police told them that he was caught and kept in the prison. And police confiscated the sword hidden in the Bara. Constable Marathe and Gautama Gangurde laid a clever trap and caught Jaganath Pandit at his farm for the first time people responsible for committing reckless atrocities against dalits were behind bars.

Denial of Education

The dominance of the upper caste people in education is seen clearly in this novel. The school reopened Kasbe Guruji was teaching a lesson on Babasaheb Ambedkars. The news spread in the village, Narendra Patil and other people went into the school and they tore the pages of that book. Kasbe Guruji applied for transfer and felt that it was a castiest village and he felt unsafe there. And he asked to transfer him to another place. Soon the news reached villages. And they were also waiting for his transfer but God bole Guruji and Kasbe Guruji were engaged in a heated discussion that not all Hindus are castiest. Hindu religion is tolerant religion to. Then Kasbe told him that "you are right. We should consider the cow holy and the untouchable unholy. Offer milk to the poisonous snake and murder the untouchable. Is this what you call tolerance?"(36).

Even since Sonali came to Achalpur, as a new bride, she was enchanted by the sound of dholaki drums. She was married to Prabhakar and she heard the drums and went upstairs to see the dance her heart ached thinking of the sweet and sour memories of her happy college days. She was given a dance recital at the annual function and that gained a lot of fame for her and the local papers published her photographs and interviews and along her side in the paper there were Rohit (Tatya Kambles son) a dalit boy sheeven praised him and it created anger with the savarnas. She and Rohit got to know each other only in the dance and they became close friends. While the savarnas boys sent the photograph of Rohit and Sonali dance together to her father. As soon as Baliram Patil saw it he felt angry. Sonali had the habit of writing poems and many got published too and when Sonalis dairy of poems got into her fathers hand he mistook it and put an end to Sonalis education.

Religious Views

The rivalry between the upper caste and lower caste men in *Hindu* is depicted through politics. Madhukar Kavale was upset because he feared that Tatya Kamble would become the next patil. Vishnu Pujari felt that people were losing eternal faith as they were going to see jalsa and the collection of the money in the temple was becoming low and Jaganath Pandit felt that because of Tatya Kamble only he lost his job. All of them were unhappy with Tatya Kamble for one reason or other. Tatya Kamble gave speech about Ambedkar by quoting his words

> "Why do you stay in a religion that does not allow you to enter the temple? Why do you stay in a religion that does not acknowledge your Humanity? Why do you stay in a religion that does not allow you even water? A religion that forbids the treatment of human as human is not a

> religion but nacked domination. A religion in which touching of unclean animal is permitted but touching of human is prohibited is not a religion but insanity" (50, 51).

Dalits now converted to Buddhism. They had thrown away the idols of the Hindu god and goddesses on to the garbage. Dalits were following new faiths and new ways of worship. Milands house though still of Hindu idols. His wife Lakshmi stealthily worships them. When an activist comes to their home the idols are to be hidden. His living room represents the portraits of Babasaheb and Buddha, and the kitchen belongs to Hindu god and goddesses.

> "Whenever I feel weak and helpless, I stand before the Hindu gods and goddesses with folded hands. And when I am bloated with self-confidence and dreaming of revolution, I go and stand with a bowed head before Babasaheb Ambedkars and Gautama Buddhas figurines"(6).

The school reopened Kasbe Guruji was teaching a lesson on Babasaheb Ambedkars. The news spread in the village, Narendra Patil and other people went into the school and they tore the pages of that book. Kasbe Guruji applied for transfer and felt that was a castiest village and he felt unsafe there. And he asked to transfer him to another place. Soon the news reached villages. And they were also waiting for his transfer but God bole Guruji and Kasbe Guruji were engaged in a heated discussion that not all Hindus are castiest. Hindu religion is tolerant religion to. Then Kasbe told him that "you are right. We should consider the cow holy and the untouchable unholy. Offer milk to the poisonous snake and murder the untouchable. Is this what you call tolerance?"(36). Then God boles stop came and he got down.

One evening Tatya Kamble programmed about the dhamma chakra parivarthan, the day Dr. Ambedkars and thousands of dalits converted to Buddhism began with everyone praying to Buddha. Tatya Kamble gave speech about Ambedkar by quoting his words

> "Why do you stay in a religion that does not allow you to enter the temple? Why do you stay in a religion that does not acknowledge your Humanity? Why do you stay in a religion that does not allow you even water? A religion that forbids the treatment of human as human is not a religion but nacked domination. A religion in which touching of unclean animal is permitted but touching of human is prohibited is not a religion but insanity" (50, 51).

Kabir Kamble felt that everyone should convert their religion from Hindu to Buddhism. But the idea turned him very somber "We have depended on the savarnas for our daily bread even after conversion. Our God will chang, our rituals of worship will change but the question regarding dal roti wont change. Complete transformation is not possible until the economic slavery of the dalits is washed away.

Sufferings of Women

After the murder of Tatya Kamble the Dalits were scattered in different places because of fear they were hidden in the fields to save their life. Manikchand and Gopichand with Miland went to their farm house and they were least bothered about the murder. Even though the muderd of the Dalit pricked Miland as they belong to the same caste he was not able to react to the situation as he was in company with the upper caste men of the night. Gopichand and Manikchand got a Dalit girl hidden in the fields and they wanted to rape her. Miland opened the latch of the restroom and he heard sound of women s anklet. Both of them were dragging her resisting body. They disrobed her she pleaded them to leave her. While Miland asked them to leave her because she was a dalit women and she came into the fields to save her life. And now you are killing her. For which they said shewas a women. And they were men and why do you seek caste even in sex? He pushed him out of the bedroom. He was angry he couldnt break doors like hero and save her. Gopichand left Manikchand in the bedroom with her and came out. Later Gopichand went inside. Then it was Miland turns to get into the room after Gopichand, Miland went into the room he saw her she was a new bride. He gave her sari and asked her to go. If he was an activist he must have told the truth to people. He felt shameful for his deed. The last night incident still remained in Milands mind. His head ached like a wound filled with pus. He thought of the young bride and he felt that would she go and tell others about the rape or will she remain quite.

Miland was on his way to the hospital to see his wife lakshmi for second delivery. In the bus stop he was attracted to a women and he felt to have sex with her though his wife was not in home but when he went near her he came to know that it was Surekha and he knew her business and her husband was in jail so he ran away at full speed. Then he went to hospital and he came to know that lakshmi was given birth to a girl child but he expected boy but it was a great disappointment to him and he thought of his debts then he met Gopichand and Manikchand and got money from him.

A grand pooja was performed in the temple. Dalit lady Draupadi reached the temple after sweeping the village streets. Vishnu Pujari had his eyes on her. She asked for Prasad and Vishnu Pujari told her to come inside the temple to get it she told that her place is near the steps how can a Mahra come into the temple. But still he asked her to get into the temple and when she entered into the temple he grabbed her she tried to release herself from his grip by shouting and later on Sudhakar entered the temple and she ran away and Vishnu Pujari face fell for the deed he has committed. Vishnu Pujari in order to take revenge on Draupati he told Sadashiv that he has doubt on Draupathi as she doesnt come to the temple and she never gets Prasad to. And later in the afternoon he collected some stones and he went on the roof and he casted the stones on some houses. Everyone in the village came out and Sadashiv More told people that it was Draupathi who did the black art and they went straight to her house she was stripped naked and she was taken around the village naked. The draupathi in Mahabharata was not stripped naked. But draupathi in independent India was naked because she was dalit. The Bhimnagar people picked draupathi up and went. The village watched all this like blind Dhritarashtra.

Love and Marriage

Even since Sonali came to Achalpur, as a new bride, she was enchanted by the sound of dholaki drums. She was married to Prabhakar and she heard the the drums and went upstairs to see the dance. Prabhakar also accompanied her. Sudhakar too came upstairs with his mother Kashibai. And Kashibai informed Prabhakar that they have to go and visit Madhukar in pune. Then at last the couples were left to be alone in the stairs together. Then he asked about her passion towards dance and music. For which she told about Tatya Kambles dance and his fathers tamasha was good and she liked it a lot and they both went and slept together but her heart ached thinking of the sweet and sour memories of her happy college days. She was given a dance recital at the annual function and that gained a lot of fame for her and the local papers published her photographs and interviews and along her side in the paper there were Rohit a dalit boy she even praised him and it created anger with the savarnas. She and Rohit got to know each other only in the dance and they became close friends. While the savarnas boys sent the photograph of Rohit and Sonali dance together to her father. As soon as Baliram Patil saw it he felt angry. Sonali had the habit of writing poems and many got published too and when Sonalis dairy of poems got into her father s hand he mistook it and put an end to Sonalis education.

References

1. Limbale, Sharankumar. (2004). Towards the Aesthetics of Dalit literature: History, Controversies and considerations. Orient Black Swan, Hyderabad.
2. Nimbalkar, Waman. (2006). Dalit literature: Nature and Role. Prabodhan Prakashan, Nagpur.

Chapter - XII

Caste, Sub-Caste and Gender issues in Bama's Vanmam - Vendetta: A Study

It is an unfortunate fact that women in India reality face inequality and marginalisation in terms of education, job opportunities, pay and health. Women are being haunted by crime and violence due to various reasons. If it is the case of the Dalit and Tribal women, they have been discriminated in every walk of their life. The proposition of the present paper is to portray the experiences of sufferings and oppression faced by the Dalit women not only by elite sections but also within their own community. As marginalisation is the powerlessness and exclusion experienced by a group, resulting from an inequality of control of resources and power structures within society. In an attempt to explore the position of women in the society, the paper deals with the key aspects of caste discrimination, gender violence and identity crises with reference to Bama s *Vanmam-Vendetta* (2008).

I

The hardships of Dalit women are not simply due to their poverty, economical status, or lack of education, but are a direct result of the severe exploitation and suppression by the upper classes, which is legitimized by Hindu religious scriptures (Thind; Agarwal). Dr. B. R. Ambedkar, an architect of the Indian constitution, also makes it very clear in his article titled "The rise and fall of Hindu woman" that the root causes of suffering for women in India are these so called Hindu religious books (Thind; Agarwal). According to the Hindu caste hierarchy, there are four castes namely the Brahmins (priestly caste), the Kshatriya (warriors), the Vaishyas (traders) and the Shudras (menial task workers). Below this, four tier caste ladder is another rung; they are called the untouchables (Panchamas). Among the untouchables, the status of women is further eroded and closely linked to the concept of purity. This is what the rigid, fundamentalist Hindupromotes through continuation of caste system, imposing the Brahmincal values to maintain the caste system. According to the Manusmriti, women have no right to education, independence, or wealth. It not only justifies the treatment of Dalit women as a sex object but also justifies a number of violent atrocities on women as can be seen in the following verses (Agarwal; Manusmitri):

Her father protects (her) in childhood, her husband protects (her) in youth, and her sons protect (her) in old age; a woman is never fit for independence. (Manusmriti IX.3)

Women are not given freedom and they lack their individuality and so, they are forced to rely upon the men for each and every thing in life and accordingly they are being oppressed and treated very low. Even the killing of a Dalit woman is explicitly justified as a minor offence for the Brahmins: equal to the killing of an animal (Manusmitri). If the killing of an untouchable was justified as a minor offence, you can imagine the treatment they received throughout their lives. The worst exploitation of Dalit women involves a lifetime of suffering, torture, and rape (Thind). Justified by the Vedic scriptures, the Devdasi system (also known as temple prostitution) was introduced by the High caste Hindus, and it still exists in some parts of India (Thind; Agarwal; Narula). The only way these Dalit women can escape the viscous cycle of poverty, abuse and oppression is through education. Through education more Dalit women can come to know their basic human rights and they can then raise an even stronger voice against abuse and exploitation from the upper castes (Thind; Agarwal).

The novel "*Vanmam-Vendetta* [vengeance, revenge] (2008) written by Bama portrays the animosity between two castes within Dalits. Pallars and Parayas are the two Dalit Casts discussed in the text. Pallars identified themselves as Hindus and Parayas are mostly Christian converts. A small rift between them caused by the upper class people make the women suffer and later how the women manage to lead their life without the help of men and how they speak out bravely to the police about the murder and injustice happened to them shows the strength of the women in the novel. It is very pertinent to know that Women are subjugated in every sphere of life both by men of upper caste and by her own men. Gail Omvedt, renowned Dalit studies scholar, has said the following in her review of Vanmam: "In almost every region of India there are two main (Dalit) castes, often at odds." (Indian Express, New Delhi, August 9, 2008). The concept of the novel is how the land owners of the dominated "Naicker" caste stroke the fire between Pallars and Parayas to preserve Naickers own status.

Bama states that a village situated in south Tamilnadu and the real life events that took place in it inspired me to write the novel Vanmam in 2002. Marginalised people, those who have been pushed to the very edges of society, have put aside their internal enmities if they are to reclaim their self-respect and their rightful place in the society.

II

When each caste tries to uplift their social status in the society the women are being humiliated and oppressed by other men and by their own men. The rift between the pallars and Parayars leads to the suffering of women in the village and they are being torchered by the police and they are left in their houses without the men. These women try to manage their food and lead their life without the help of their men. They voice out bravely for the murder that the Pallars did for the Parayars. Vanmam documents the hatred and vengeance among the various Dalit communities, an area too touchy to be addressed and too complex to be grasped. It is sad but true that the graded inequality that sustains caste order is replicated among the Dalits as well.

The idyllic bonding between the two communities built through cultural events, sports and celebration of festivals turns out to be a mere facade to mask the burning jealousies over socio-economic issues. Unfortunately, conversion to Christianity becomes the key variable in causing this divide. The bloody caste clashes begin with a Hindu Pallar murdering a Christian Parayar. The story ends with the murder of an innocent Parayar, which leads to the dawn of realisation among both the parties about how they have been made pawns in the hands of caste Hindus.

In the village of Kandampatti, where the novel is set, the people have been living for years with the burden of fears of their fellowmen, and of what the future may bring. Due to these unnecessary rivalries with dalits the young men are forced to live in hiding. Children cannot go to school, women are widowed and children are orphaned. The loss on both sides makes them realize the role of dominant castes and state machinery especially the police in perpetrating their animosity. The story ends when yet another killing of an innocent parayar by the agitated pallars leads to a serious rethink in both caste groups. They realize that the dominant castes have been following a divide and rule strategy to keep the fires of Vanmam-Vendetta burning between the two castes. The parayars and the pallars confess and decide to sink their differences put the past behind them and show a united front at the panchayat poles. United they are and make history by capturing power for the very first time from the entrenched dominant caste leadership. Vendetta has many faces and takes many forms.

III

Kandampatti village is a big place. People of many different castes reside there. The parayars live in the eastern part of the village. Next to them the four or five streets are occupied by the pallar houses. Some distance away from the parayar and pallar houses are the kakkalayar houses. In about four or five streets are the weaver chaliyars, the moopanars, and pannadis. (pg:5). The eastern part of the village belongs to the lower caste people and the western part of the village belongs to the upper caste people like Thevars, Chettiars, Aasaris, Pillais, Nadars, Naickers. The Parayars took the landlords farm land on lease and toiled hard day and night to turn every barren land into fertile land. The parayars were well educated. They did many jobs now a day. The women do their part too. This fumigated the upper caste people.

The Naickers muttered something among themselves in Telugu. At one time they were starving without even gruel, and now look at their power! And their clothes! Even better than what our own childrens wear. When theyre at the bus stand, we cant even tell who they are. Also, both the men and women of their caste are getting educated. All this is coming from their religion. The pallans are better; at least theyre still respectful towards us. (19)

The growth of the lower caste people brings hatred and vengeance into the heart of upper caste people. They dont want the parayars and pallars to grow. And they discuss that"Gone are those days when people would do jobs for you even without your having telling them" (19). The parayars were well educated and they were in different professions the village parayars were very active and had the wisdom of education. And they followed Christianity hence the Naickers wanted to bring a rift between the pallars and parayars as pallars belong to Hindu they put forth the issue of religion and the Naickers instigated the pallars and made them to be mere puppets in the hands of them stating that they all belonged to Hindu religion and the parayars belonged to the Christianity. Likewise the Naickers incited and goaded the pallans.

You know the old saying, "if the village is split into two, only the mischief- maker will celebrate". It is true instead of being sensible and cooperating, the pallans and the parayars are confronting one another with weapons drawn. Naturally the other caste people are only too delighted to stand by and watch. (63)

After the inauguration of the Ambedkar statue in the village the continuous events brought forth many problems within the parayar and pallar community and it went to the extent of murdering sesurathnam it was a gang murder in a bazaar by the pallars. On hearing all these news, policeman came to both the streets, and the men folk of both streets fled. As for the pallar street women, they had already left their homes and gone away to stay with their people nearby villages. But the parayar street women were still in their houses. There were rumors that the pallar had killed ten parayars and the parayars had finished off five pallars. There was panic everywhere. No one knew for certain who had been killed, and by whom.

IV

The women in the Parayar Street were taken to the police station by policemen who told them that collector is waiting in the bus stand and so they were forced to get into the van and they were kept in lock up. The police havent brought any women from pallar street this made the women to wail and shout at the police men. Many women have left their six month old child in the cradle and all the men have flied to different place to escape from the clutches of the police men. The women in the cell wept and made loud wail.

"Who is going to come... What can they say...how can they get us released? No ones left in our streets. Do we have to rot here forever? asked Rosamma in tears." (85). These women were innocent and they were not aware of the situation. Chellakili was begged the police guard, Ayya, youve brought all of us here by playing a cruel trick on us and locked us up like this. We have just returned from our daily jobs, and everything has been left undone at home. What crime we done that you have locked us up like this? We dont even know the detail of what happened in the village, ayya.(85). The inspector came the next day and released the old women and mother of the infants but chellakili and other sixteen women were locked up into the cell again. As they were being escorted back, one of the policemen kicked chellakili in the lower belly with his boots and said "so you complained to the circle inspector about us, eh? Well rip up your mouth if you utter another word!"(pg86). Another policeman hit her hard on her lower back with his lathi. Chellakilli curled up and collapsed on the floor of the cell. "As she lay there on the floor of that police lock-up, she felt a sharp pain in her belly... And ...she had an abortion right there. She had lost her baby. What agony Chellakili suffered..." (86). After seven years she was carrying her baby but the policeman has kicked her and the baby. The women around Chellakili consoled her.

There were no men left in the Parayar Street only few women were there and they were determined to take the corpse of their men and clear it. Rosemary drove the cart and brought the corpse. "The women gathered together, took the bodies in the cart to the graveyard, dug a big grave all by themselves, and buried all three bodies in that single grave" (87). The policemen were astonished to see the women doing the burial themselves. "these she- donkeys have so much guts, eh, they remarked" "(87) The next day policemen went into the Parayar street and started beating the women with lathis chasing them as they ran and raining blows on them, and cursing them in the foulest language. They entered every street and every house thrashing all the women by asking about their hidden husbands. Thirty or forty of the policemen went around entering every single house, dragging the women out into the street, and beating them up. With no regard even for the infants and aged. When the police stopped beating the women the women, who were hurt horribly, swollen with bruises all over, sat and cried. “Even our husbands have never beated us like this. Are these fellows beasts from the jungle... are they drunk and mad... how can they hit us like this... see how the blood has clotted and turned black...” wailed Irudaya Mary loudly (89). The men of both pallar and parayar clang were dispersed to various places, some of them were in nearby villages, some were in the forest and some went in search of new jobs to distant places to safe guard themselves. While the women were left all alone in the streets and they managed by milking the cow and distributing to other women and they were leading their life with the little food they had and they never went out for any work. Even to go to market they have to cross the pallar street. The upper caste people were basking in this issue of the lower caste. Slowly the life returned into normal.

Both the pallars and parayars started coming into the village and started leading a normal life. But still there were little vengeance among the people. The village higher official (*nattamai*) of both the caste planned to meet and sort out the issue:

> In those days the Pallars and Parayars used to be united...No accusation or anything. They used to address our people as “mama” and “machaan”, and we also used to talk to them thats the way... fooling around...having a good time. Look whats happening today... Like snakes and mongooses we are! So much hatred, jealousy, bitterness... all this is happening only in our village. Even if there are any quarrels we should settle them peacefully (121).

Both the caste people gathered and talked among them and Pallars asked the Parayars not to show the witness of the Pallars murders to the police and so the Parayars accepted and from then on they were in unity.

And the village people spoke:

Let them say whatever they want to. We should not retrace our steps. What is past is past. But the children who are yet to be born must be able to live in this village. So lets trust one another and try to get along together. We must be our guard in case anyone tries to provoke us and create enmity between our two castes (130).

This was the constant message from the elders of both streets. Later on after the amicable situation of both the castes the upper class people mocked at them "what sort of fellows are these? After so much killing... So much wandering around like refugees...theyre supposed to be united again. Shameless fellows!" (133).

Later on the people of Pallar and Parayar decided that they would nominate a person to from their own caste to contest in election against the Naickers. It caused much heart burn among the Naickers. They nominated Kaalaiyan from the pallar caste. He won the panchayat president election in kandampatti. Then the people of the both caste said that "its not enough that we have won in this Panchayat election. The Dalit voice must resonate in the state legislatures and in the national parliament...As Ambedkar, the champion of the downtrodden, said, we must capture the levers of government power. Let this be the first step towards goal." (134). From then on the Parayars and Pallars remained determined that whatever anyone might say they would never fight again and only time can heal the wounds they said and lived together in mutual tolerance and friendship.

V

On the whole, Bamas *Vanmam - Vendetta* gives a message about their community not about individuality, about revolt not about passivity, about progress not about backwardness.

This message is to the entire world about their status in society by portraying the exploitive, helpless, and en- grossed with grief, suppressed and enslaved and a subaltern state. The text also portrays how the Dalit women face many sufferings by other men and by their own men. Education gives them knowledge and changes their way of living.

References

1. Agarwal, S, "*Genocide of women in Hinduism*", Sudrastan Books, Jabalpur 1999 Print. <http://www.geocities.com/realitywithbite/hindu.htm retrieved on 8th Sept 2007>
2. Bama, *Vanmam-Vendetta* Translated from Tamil by Seshadri Malini, Oxford University press, New Delhi, India 2008 Print.
3. <http://www.jagarannepal.org>
4. <http://sivanagaiah.blogspot.in>
5. Manu, Manu Smriti. *The laws of Manu with the Bhasya of Medhatithi.* Translated by Ganga Natha Jha, University of Calcutta, Calcutta, India.1920 Print.
6. Narula. S., *Broken People: Caste Violence against India's Untouchables.* London: Human Rights Watch, 1999. Print.
7. News Archives. <http://www.ambedkar.org>
8. Thind, G. S., *Our Indian Sub-Continent Heritage.* Cross-town Press, LTD. British Columbia, Canada. 2000 Print.
9. Sawant B.Siddhartha, *An Era of Dalit literature An Explosion of Muffled Voices,* International Referred Research Journal, January, 2012. ISSN- 0974-2832, RNI-RAJBIL 2009/29954; VoL.III ISSUE-36.

Chapter - XIII

Education as a tool for the Emancipation of Youths: A Study of Dalit life

The awakening of the lower caste for the emergence of the idea of liberty, social justice, and equality ignited the Dalits to begin the Dalit movements in India it is a collective agitation against the caste, creed, cultural and social exploitation to fight against the atrocities upon them from the age old tradition of Hinduism to get a new self image and new identity. Education plays a key role in the development for the empowerment of the Dalits. It is through education the Dalits were able to voice out against the atrocities and discrimination which the caste Hindus imposed on them. The Dalits were not able to fight with the higher caste people instead they used the pen as sword to question the ideologies imposed on them. Education has played a vital role in the development of the Dalits and it was through education the real emancipation of the Dalits began in India. It broke the chains of caste and social exclusion. The proposition of the paper will deal with the how the education has paved way for the development of the Dalits and what are the changes that took place in the life of the marginalised people after gaining education.

Key words: Education, Dalits, Equality, Justice, Empowerment.

Dalits are the people who are economically, politically and socially exploited and are forced to live as untouchables outside the village doing all the low level jobs offered to them by the privileged people of the society. They were not allowed to live a life with dignity they were treated as the suppressed class of Indian society. In Indian constitution the Dalits come under the category of scheduled caste. They are given different names like asyu, Dasa, Atisudra, Panchama, Tirukulattar, Adikarnataka, Adi Dravida Pariahs, Chamars, Mahars, Bhangis etc. State wise they claimed different name as Mahars in Maharastra, Malas and Madigas in Andhra,Holeyas in Karnataka, Chamars in Western North India, Pallar and Paraiyans in Tamil Nadu. The minority Aryans who settled in the river of Ganges defeated the majority indigenous Dalits. Hindu scriptures and religious texts treated Dalits as slaves. Caste was not God created ideas but it was manmade ideologies to suppress and to dominate the other which is deeply rooted in the Indian Hindu tradition.

The privileged Brahmin was treated with high respect and had the superior power in hand and the less privileged Dalits were treated equal to animals and mere slaves. Vedas are ruling the Hindu religion even now and the Brahmins considered themselves as pure and Gods people which were totally done on the basis of the karma and dharma done in the previous birth. They considered the Dalits as impure and low by birth. The Brahmin speaks about punarjanma which mean re-birth and they propose a rule towards the Dalit and make them believe that their situation as a slave is due to the adharma done by them in the previous birth and they have to obey the Brahmins and do all the odd jobs imposed to them in order to attain a prosperous birth next time.

Lack of knowledge made the Dalits to believe the Brahmins and the Brahmins made them believe that the only God who will help them attain salvation is Brahmins so they have to obey them and follow their words and should consider them equal to God. Dalit are denied to enjoy the mankinds basic needs and rights such as food, shelter, clothing and they have to depend on the dominant class to do all the agricultural and other labour work in order to have their livelihood.

The dominant caste created the rule in the form of religion and they considered themselves high and the sight, shadow, touch of the Dalits were considered as impure but the Dalit did all the odd works in their field, cleaned the household, brought firewood to cook, washed their clothes etc in spite of all these things the Brahmins considered them as untouchables. The exploited classes included all the people who do all the odd jobs in at the lower level in the society and they are named as the Scheduled Caste by the government.

Dalit were not exposed to the Vedas and Hindu religious texts they were made to blindly follow the law created by the Brahmins and their writings in the Hindu religion in the form of God and the Brahmins were well aware that if the Dalits were made to read the Hindu text they know the reality that they will not obey them and so they were deprived of the education.

Dalit movement was organised with the strength of Dalit literary movement as they had only pen to fight against the social inequalities. There writing started in the times of Mukti movement and it flourished into various genres in the time of Dalit Panther movement which started in 1970s with the influence of Black Panther movement from the west. These writings were to break the long silence of the dalits of thousand years they found the space to express their revolt against the social evil imposed on them for centuries. Majority of writers who wrote the brahminical text wrote with a Brahmin touch in order to sustain their mode of living in the society and they occupied the upper positions and leaving the dalits to do the lower job by subjugating them from the top in the form of religion, birth, caste etc.

The pioneers of many Dalit movements were commoners and they brought about a great radical and revolutionary change in the life of the Dalits as the upper caste people never realised about their hard work and stole the fruit of the poor so the importance of movement played a surgical role in the society. Non-brahmin movement, Satyashodhak Samaj, and Self-Respect influenced the people of Maharashtra and Madras, Arya samaj influenced the Punjab by initiating the Ad-Dharm movement, Brahmo Samaj instigated the Namashudra and Adi-Andhra movememt and in Kerala the Ezhava were influenced by Narayana Guru likewise the Dalits initiated various movements in different states. Through the movements the Dalits broke the caste imposed ideologies and they broke down the restriction like taking water in the common well and water tanks, bathing in the river of the upper caste. Most important things that changed the ideology are the Mahad tank satyagraha of 1927 which lead to burn the Manusmriti, satyagraha of parvati temple in Nasik from 1930-35 and in kerala vaikom temple road satyagraha 1930-32. They no more were slaves to the Hindu people they rebelled against the oppression and subjugation of the upper caste.

Kancha Ilaiah points out two aspects of knowledge. They are: the oppressor's knowledge and the knowledge of the oppressed. Ilaiah considers Brahma's knowledge is the oppressor's knowledge:

> The Dalitbahujans have their own knowledge, reflected in several of the ideas of the Charvakas (Dalitbahujan materialists) of the ancient period. The ancient Brahmins hegemonised their knowledge and marginalised the knowledge of the Dalitbahujan Charvakas, using the image of Brahma. Brahma, thus represented the Brahmin patriarchs, and Saraswathi represented the Brahmin women who had been turned into sexual objects. (28)

The Dalits are sent to school and what is taught to them in class is different from the life they face:

> Childhood formations are important for a person-female or male-to become a full human being. But our childhoods

were mutilated by constant abuse and by silence, and by a stunning silence at that. There was the conspiracy to suppress the formation of our consciousness...Even after schools were opened to us because of independence or swaraj, a word which even today I fail to understand, the school teacher was against us, the textbook language was against us. Our homes have one culture and the schools have another culture...The gap between the two was enormous. There was no way in which one resembled the other. In fact these two cultures were poles apart. (30)

Caste is the major factor in education

Uma Chakravarthy argues that, The monopoly of the upper castes, scared knowledge, book knowledge, intellectual inquiries, like astronomy, were superior. The lower castes, who labored, developed and preserved the knowledge of agriculture, of plants, animals, domestic livestock, weather, soil, pests, tools used in goldsmith, fishing and hunting are not considered as skilled professionals. Even the crafts skill, one of the primitive skills of the Dalits which is also implied knowledge of the materials used like metals, wood, clay bamboo, reed and bricks is also considered as an outsider's profession. (31)

Religious conversion helped dalits to learn as the missionaries established schools in the late 19th and 20th centuries. Many students joined and gained knowledge. Ambedkar's involvement in Indian socio-political scenario made a major mark in Dalits, lives across the country. Ambedkar gave more importance to educate the Dalits. His clarion call, educates, organize and agitate, made an indelible impression in Dalits lives. Before him it was Phule who fought for the education of Dalits and he established schools especially for Dalit students. He was pioneer to start school for the Dalit girls too.

First of all the Dalits belong to the lower strata of the society and they are unaware about the importance of education. Secondly the distance between the school and their living is far and they dont make necessary move to pursue education. Thirdly it is the elite class people who are the teachers and they may treat the Dalits differently and it is the main reason for the drop outs of the Dalits in higher education level. Fourthly the Dalits are unaware of the government policies and schemes for the developmentand even though they become aware of it the institutions dont support them to reach it. The major drawback is poverty their life depend on daily wages and they send their children to work as laboures for leading daily life.

The government schemes for Elementary Education are: Sarva Shiksha Abhiyan, Mid Day Meal, Strengthening of Teachers Training Institute Schemes for Infrastucture Development of Private Aided/Unaided Minority Institutes (IDMI), Mahila Samakhya, Strengthening for providing quality Education in Madrassas (SPQEM).

The schemes for the emancipation of education for Dalits in Secondary Education are: Rashtriya Madhyamik Shiksha Abhiyan (RMSA), Inclusive Education for Disable at Secondary Stage (IEDSS), Incentives to Girls at Secondary Stage, National Merit cum Means Scholarship, Financial Assistance for Appointment of language Teachers, Adolescence Education Programme, Girls Hostel, Model School, ICT at School, Vocationalisation of Secondary Education, Model School Under Public- Private Partnership(PPP)Mode.

Various schemes for Adult Education are: Saakshar Bharat, State Resource Center (SRCs), Jan Shikshan Sansthans(JSSs), Assistance to Voluntary Agencies.

Schemes for University and Higher Education are: Rashtriya Ucchatar Shiksha Abhiyan (RUSA), National Initiative for Design Innovation, National Research Professorship (NRP), Establishment of New Central Universities, Indira Gandhi National Tribal University, Establishment of 14 World Class Central Universities, Setting up of 374 Degree Colleges in Educationally Backward Districts, Scheme for incentivising state governments for expansion of higher education institutions, New central sector scheme of interest subsidy on educational loans taken by students from economically backward sections to pursue technical/professional education in India under the educational loan scheme of the Indian banks association, Construction of girls hostels, Supporting uncovered state universities and colleges, Additional assistance to about 160 already covered universities and about 5500 colleges, Strengthening science based higher education and research in universities, Inter universities research institute for policy and evaluation and Schemes Implemented through Autonomous Organisations.

It is only through education the real emancipation of the Dalits will assert to break the caste based discrimination. Dalit literature itself emerged as a new form of literature only after the advent of the Dalit Panthermovement in Maharashtra in 1970 until then the Dalits were unaware about the alphabets and texts. Being the original inhabitant of the land their lamentation, sufferings were not registered in the elite books and they were kept away from the society and from gaining knowledge. The Indian English Literature also failed to portray the life of the Dalits in their genres. Totally the lives of Dalits were unrepresented and unvoiced. To break this ideology religion acted as a tool to empower the Dalits even though as a political cause but in reality it paved way for the Dalits to gain knowledge. Government after independence established various schemes for the welfare and the development of Dalits. Today Dalit literature marks as a true form of literature through representing the Dalit lives. Dalit youths are getting empowered through education and they reform their culture, attitude and life style and strengthen their standard of living. As per the words of Ambedkar education is really a true emancipation of Dalits his vision has come true. As Nethaji stated One individual may die for an idea, but that idea will, after his death, incarnate itself in a thousand lives. So is Ambedkar to Dalits and on other hand Dalits emancipation for the movement to ignite the souls of the Dalit youths.

References

1. Bolleddu, Siva Nagaiah. (2015). Writing the Self: A Thematic Study of Dalit Autobiographies. Kalpaz Publication, New Delhi, pp.1-200
2. Chakravarti, Uma. (2006). Gendering Caste: Through a Feminist Lens. Street, Kolkata, pp. 1-100.
3. Dangle, Arjun. (1994). Poisoned Bread: Translations from Modern Marathi Dalit Literature. Orient Black Swan, Mumbai, pp. 1-325.
4. Limbale, Sharankumar. (2004). Towards the aesthetics of dalit literature: history, controversies and considerations. Orient Black Swan, Hyderabad, pp. 1-40.
5. Nimbalkar, Waman. (2006). Dalit literature: Nature and Role. Prabodhan Prakashan, Nagpur, pp. 1-53.

Chapter - XIV

Representing the life of a Dalit: A Study of G. Kalyan Rao's Untouchable Spring

The life of a Dalit is always pitiful and they lack in the basic needs like food, shelter and clothes. Being the original inhabitant of the land the Dalits lost their rights and self-respect. They were demeaned in the name of religion and caste. Dalit as a community has their own culture, religion, language and lifestyle. Though they were not powerful in the initial days by writing scriptures but they had a powerful art form. The art form was two sided one side it provided the form of entertainment and on the other side it asserted the minds of the Dalits. Through street plays, Jalsas, folk dance, drama and songs the Dalits had strong messages to be conveyed to their people with rich oral tradition. Through Dalit literature the unrepresented silence is voiced out and the writers are bringing out the real life of a Dalit into light their pain and suffering are brought out to make the people realize that how human being was so mean to do injustice to his own fellow being. The preposition of the paper will deal with the life of mala and madiga the Dalits of Andhra Pradesh through the novel Untouchable Spring. Their rich art forms, discrimination, sufferings faced are being registered in this paper.

Key words: Dalits, Poverty, folk art, discrimination.

Untouchable Spring (2000) was written in Telugu and later it was translated into English by...In this novel G. Kalyan

Rao revels the sufferings and pains of the Dalits with seven generations of history. That was where Reubens father Yellanna was born he grew up sang songs and danced. Yellanna did not write songs he knew no alphabet. "All he had was a feeling heart, a sharable experience, tear-shedding eyes, swelling nerve, a turbulent blood-stream... that was it, the song would weave itself." (6) They called him singing Yelladu, dancing Yelladu but his fathers sister Boodevi called him Yellanna. Yellanna was a great artist. Reuben was born in a great artists family. Now Ruth is an heir to that family. When Yellanna sings the moving tune that combined untouchablity and hunger would be heard. The place where those who belonged to the four castes lived was *ooru.* The place where malas lived – *malapalli,* where the madigas lived- *madigapalli* and all these parts put together formed Yennela Dinni.

Yellanna was born like everyone. "Oh, you upper caste people! I, an untouchable, am walking on your pure, regal paths. Move aside. Move aside". (7) He announced his birth like anyone else. Like each ones birth touching one fathers heart, his too, touched his fathers heart. A male, he shouted out to the caste elder. He filled with caste elders stomach with toddy and felt elated. They named the child after his grandfathers name.

When *Yerra gollalu* came to the ooru there was excitement all over because they would put up street plays for ten to fifteen days in a row. Boodevi was crazy for *Chenchu Natakam* she would go to play taking her nephew along. Karanams and Kapus would sit close to the performers. Behind them, people from the washerman, barber and potter castes would sit. The malas would sit on the mala mound. The madigas would sit on the madiga mound. Those two groups would be far away from the arena. Sitting like that they would not be visible to the village elders and the elders of the other caste. The play would not begin till the Karanam and Kapus arrived. After they arrived they would praise him on skies. Then the *sutradhara* would begin the performance. Yellanna would say to his aunty that he cannot see the play she would get up and lift him and if the Karanam and kapus see her standing that would be in trouble. But she dare to stand for her nephew because of the play he would sacrifice his sleep. He asked his aunty that can he sit near the yerra gollalu but she refused in spite of her reusal Yellanna went near the performing stage and he stood and after sometime he found some people staring at him. When they came to know he was from mala they started attacking him they pelted stones on him he ran for his life. He jumped into the water and reached the shore and only then he knew that there was no waist cloth he started walking on the path. There he saw a crowd and he entered into it and they were singing dancing and applying vermillion all over the body and Yellanna applied vermillion and he to danced on when he shouted Urumula Naganna turned and saw and it was Yellanna it was nude Siva. When he asked about him he said that he was a mala and he is from Yennela Dinni. Then he collapsed to the floor. When he woke up he asked which place he was in and Urumula Naganna said it was Pakkela Dinni.

Yellanna was sleeping but Urumula Naganna was not able to sleep Yellannas arrival seemed to have caused some turmoil in him. It was three days since Naganna came to Pakkela Dinni. Urumala dancers were leaving but Naganna stayed to collect money and go he did not know what to do with Yellanna. He woke him up and gave his dress and food and he asked him about his past and he narrated the whole story with tears. Dharamaram Urumula Naganna was famous not only in Anantapuram but also in the coastal areas. It was Urumula Chandrappa who had taught Naganna the nuances of playing the Urumulu. He told him the secrets of puranas. He gave him to the world as Urumula Naganna and went away. Naganna had a special place in Ruths memories the same intensity of rage Reuben experienced when he spoke about Yellanna. In reality Chandrappa is like Sinnabba fathers younger brother. But when he was about to die he told Naga to call him Appa and he shouted at him calling Appa and he passed away smiling. The left out money of the Chandrappa was distributed among the troop and he formed a new troop and he gained a name as Rayalaseema. Urumula Nagannas voice,dance was remarkable and he knew numerous secrets of purunas and he outsmart any learned person. As soon as he heard that Yellanna was mala and he was from Yennela Dinni he remembered the hurt that the past has inflicted. Naganna has been born in Yennela Dinni, his father Narigadu and mother Latchimi also was born there. He tells about the days he spent with his mother and father in Yennela Dinni. The palm tree has been entwined with the lives of mother and father. Nagannas childhood was spent among the palm tree by eating the kernel and drinking the palm juice and being in the shade of tumma groves of Yennela Dinni. Yellanna said he was Yerrenkadus son and nephew to Boodevi. When Yerrenkadu was a small boy at that time even Boodevi was not born. Yerrenkadus father was working as a watchman at the elder karanams mango grove. It was a kind of bonded labour.

In Yennela Dinni these wretched people s lives remained mere desire. They were distraught and ruined due to their desires. It just happened with father Narigadu. There was heavy rain and continuous storm in the place mala and madigas would almost be covered by water it was at time the people gathered and talked about going to mound where upper caste people lived. The father took Naganna on his hip and mother placed the basket on her hand. "If you want to live, come along. Whoever comes in the way will be the targets of this axe... those who want to live, come along... well die anyway... Yellamma too has been submerged. Come, come, you coward bastards... come on, you..." (32) The people started following him. "For the first time, the untouchable storm fell on the ooru. For the first time inthe Yellena Dinni, so many malas and madigas were walking amidst houses of upper caste, on their paths, in the middle of the ooru, crossing the lanes of the temple... walking towards the mound." (32) They were on top of the mound at higher level than upper caste. They had confidence that they will not die. In the morning it appeared as if malapalli and madigapalli was washed away. Whatever they carried they cooked and they ate. The water has wiped out malapalli and madigapalli. That day no one had food to eat it was getting dark father was missing and in the night the four people came on the heads with bags full of rice they broke the sahukars shop and now people would gather and they would be talking only about us. They started cooking the rice and they ate greedily. The people spoke "They tell us not to live on heights. The stream tells us not to live on low-lying areas. If we come to the top, theyll kill us. If we are in the lower areas, the stream will kill us. No matter what, death is inescapable. But... listen... listen to our words. We arent born only to die." (35) Naganna could not sleep he was awake listening to the conversations of the elders. The nest day it was normal nothing happened but in the evening the people carried a corpse and it was the death of his father.

People cried aloud and they knew who was behind the murder. A month after fathers death it became necessary to bid farewell to Yennela Dinni. When he was leaving Yennela Dinni he cried a lot. He felt uneasy leaving father, palm trees, ridges of the rice field, crabs running, tumms grove and everything else. He felt as if his childhood came to an end in Yennela Dinni. Then he came to know Urumula Chandrappa and they drove in the cart and got down in Dharmaram as it was the birth place of Chandrappa and they stayed there and he grew to marriage age and he got married to Ramulu after his marriage his mother bid him farewell and it was final farewell of her. She died on Chandrappas lap and Ramulu was pregnant and Chandrappa said that if it was a baby girl he would name it as Latchmi and if it was a boy he would name it as Naraiah. Unfortunately Chandrappa died and unable to deliver ,Ramulu also died.

From then he started performing for Gangammas songs with vermillion dance. He lost everyone in his life. When he saw Yellanna he felt like talking for some time. He felt like telling Yellanna the *Puranic* secrets. He felt like sharing witrh Yellanna the steps and movements Chandrappa has thought him. "Yennela Dinni has chased away this child only for him. Naganna thought that he had come searching for him alone. Yellanna told about Boodevi more than his father and mother and it reminded him of his childhood days he wanted to drink toddy so that he would come out fromtired and he walked towards the fields of Pakkela Dinna he saw Yellanna accompanied him and he spoke to him and asked him whether he could learn to dance. He asked him whether he would come to Dharmaram to learn Urumu. Then he went near toddy tree and he drank the toddy and he gave it to Yellanna and he told the story of his birth and when they reached malapalli the people said that they should stay there have food and collect the money and then leave home. After the meal they slept and when he woke up he caressed his feet and felt that he was the one to whom he wanted to teach his art. Yellanna got up and said that his aunty would be crying for him. Many years later Ruth heard the voice of the bird as Reuben imitated it. Ruth feels that both Yellanna and Naganna are walking together in front of her to Yennela Dinni.

In Ruths words that is a beautiful scene. It was a wonderful journey one of them is known and the other needs to be introduced. "In this country caste is more important than art. Art is also weighed in the scale of caste." (41) Ruth thinks over it again and again.

"They ploughed the fields. Made beds. Watered them. Plucked weeds.Protected the cobs. Harvested the crop. Prepared the threshing floor. Threshed the grain.Heaped them. Separated the chaff from the grain. They did everything. Half hungry, under the stars in the sky, on sand mounds, folding their knees into their bellies, they slept. They did not get hold of the fields. They did not get hold of the field beds. The grains did not belong to them. Without anything belonging to them, they rained sweat on earth. Like that, they were kept cruelly away from the fruit of their toil." (42)

The song was born from every work done on the earth. Planting, sapling, plucking weeds, harvesting the crops and laboring, the coolie mother sang. To forget hunger, to forget the child crying out for milk, to forget the pain of the bent back, the pallavi was heard from the silent voice. Reaping the harvest they sang the harvest song. "They hid life in those songs. They made them voice sexuality, humour, compassion, not artificially like great poets wrote, but very naturally like air, water , sun, moon and stars." (42) In truth the memories of Ruth are the representation of pain and hatred. "All of it happened like that. It really happened like that. Nagannas and Yellanas did not go after recognition. Didnt dance to be known. Didnt sing. Art was in their veins. In their blood.In the depths of their hearts.In their very sweat." (43) Reuben used these words repeatedly. Naganna used to think his dance was only to worship Ganga and only to please Siva. Now again Ruth thinks of the past which Reuben told her. Naganna and Yellannaentered Yennela Dinni and Naganna thought that it was the village of his childhood after many years he is steeping there. When he left he went with his mother and now he came back as a companion to Yellanna. "That day he tied his childhood in a bundle and left. Today he was coming back carrying pain and lonliness." (43)

Pittodu brought up Yellanna in a different way when Sulochannamma saw her first she said "She looks like the Karanam daughter and praised the girls colour, hair and dress."(69) Finally Pittodu accepted for the marriage and they gave three rupees and six anas as bride price and got them married. Subhdra did not come in the way of Yellanna. She got pregnant and delivered a male baby. Naganna named it as Sivaiah. They started enacting the puranas in the stage.

Naganna thought all the things which Chandrappa had thought to him. It took three months for him and the other artist to learn the dance and drama and one day they started to enact on the stage. Enacting in the stage gave them fame and but the problem came when the enactors has to ask before the play wheather the karnams has come but when Naganna and Yellanna performed they never asked but they said "Have the great pedda mala and the pedda madiga who is as great has come?" (79). The way the people reacted irritated the karnams and it became a major issue. It was a shame for them when the people reacted like this and they could not digest that change. "In their eyes, Naganna and Yellanna appeared like big criminals. They thought they ought not to swallow the heinous act of raising the mala and madiga to the level of a karanam or a kapu. They thought of teaching them both a lesson." (79)

When Atchireddys father -in-law came to visit his daughter he heard the karanam and Atchireddy talking about Atelladu. He said after listening to everything "If it were me, I would kill those two basterds" (79). When he knew that there was a performance in his place Dibbalamitta he sent word to a man of what must be done. Bukkireddy sent word to the mala and madigas elders the day before the performance. He told that "if Atelladus performance took place in Dibbalamitta both the palles would be reduced to ashes." (80) If they want to perform they should not call the pedda mala and the pedda madinga the way the karanams and kapus were called. Naganna found it strange and felt that the life was taking him on a different direction. He sent word to Polayi and Mataiahs nephew Musalaiah. All gathered and they planned to make the mala mound cultivable as the karanams used the land for bonded labour they even occupied devadasis land so these people started clearing the land of the mala only after the third day the elders in the ooru arranged the meeting karanam and Atchireddy and the other reddys gathered and when the issue was put up Naganna came forward to tell that it was he who did it and he thought to tell it to karanam when the work was over. This time in the meeting karanam found many difference in the way the people talked. The meeting ended as the karanam got up and said "Families shouldnt sit on our heads. But they arent clearing up the malas mound for families to live, right?" (87) The malas and madigas made the malas mound cultivable. They shared the piece of land with each other. They ought to remember Narigadu and Mataiah. Their sacrifice, courage, the blood they shed and the history continued like that. The karanam did not consider much for the malas land but it irritated him.

The day for the performance in Dibbalamitta was nearing and they were cautious that the people from different places came toward Dibbalamitta in order to support the karanams and reddys. Naganna felt why should he perform in the ooru by representing everyone and told that he was not a cattle in their shed to do what he wishes? The day of the performance came and it was a dilemma whether to address the gathering or to perform. "The palles did not dare have a performance addressing the elders with respect. Doing such a thing needed lot of courage. Therefore, Yellanna thought not to perform would be the best way to save self-respect."

(89) Yellanna said to the people that lets not perform now lets do it on another time. That day the walk to Yennela Dinni was very heavy. It was a great defeat to Naganna he never spoke a word. In the night he sang the song and Yellanna was with him after sometime he told that he felt sleepy and he closed the eyes and he never opened the eyes again.

"Yellanna did everything for Naganna. Till he performed everything, he remained with a strong heart. After everything was over, he felt as if nothing was left for him and everything in front of him had come to nought. He remained all alone staring in all directions. He was searching Naganna in every direction. He brought to mind every word Naganna spoke before his death." (92)

All the people from the village took advance for the performances were coming and going back he was returning the advances he was not able to perform without Naganna. Life was full of inexplicable agony, dryness, a loss that could not be filled, a thirst that could not be quenched. Yellanna became completely sage-like and dumb. Only shadows were lurking about his creativity. The relationship between the society and himself was weakening. He sang. Till now happiness and contentment alone were the reason for his singing. "How he came and how he went away! What didhe do and what did he leave undone before he went away! The Urumula mala. Yennela Dinnis Nagannas. Narigadus son, a great artist. What in fact did he search for?" (93). Narigadu, Mataiah, Naganna standing in front touching his heart, water gushing out of the eyes they were floating out every second. He sang about the story of Naganna everyone around cried he said "One brave man died a heroic death. Another brave man repaid the debt of blood of that brave man. There was land behind both these people. There was self-respect." (95) Yellanna left the village and he had no intention to come back. He roamed around and sang song which ever village he went he went first to malapalli and madingapalli and in every song he remembered Subhadra. The Dalits lived with their own rich tradition of art form their plight is represented in this novel. Till the end the Dalit personalities never gave up their self respect and dignity.

Reference

1. Kalyan Rao, G. (2010). Untouchable Spring. Orient Black Swan, Hyderabad.
2. Limbale, Sharankumar. (2004). Towards the Aesthetics of Dalit literature: History, Controversies and considerations. Orient Black Swan, Hyderabad.
3. Nimbalkar, Waman. (2006). Dalit literature: Nature and Role. Prabodhan Prakashan, Nagpur.

Index

N

O

P